CUSH TO MYSTERIOUS BABYLON

Africa and the Covenant People

BY
MICHAEL RAY LEMONS

ISBN: 979-8-9885303-3-6 (Paperback)
ISBN: 979-8-9885303-4-3 (Hardcover)

Published by:

Dedication

This book is a work of gratitude to Mary Underwood Lemons, who gave me the courage to research and challenge traditional ways of learning history. Her stories from childhood inspired me, and through her scriptural narratives, I found the confidence to write this book. My interest in American history and understanding various cultures grew, thanks to her influence. Writing didn't come naturally to me, but some stories are worth telling. Thank you, Mom, for giving me the confidence to put my thoughts into words. Without your guidance, this book wouldn't exist.

Table of Contents

Dedication .... *iii*

Acknowledgment .... *ix*

Introduction .... *xi*

Chapter One
Skin Colors: From Historical Oppression to
Global Power Structures.. 1
European Genocide in Namibia and Congo *2*
Post-WWII Changes and Independence Struggles..................... *3*

Chapter Two
Cush: The Legacy and Impact of Africa's Oldest Civilization 8
Cush's and the Kushites' Legacies *9*
Satan's Impact and Paganism *15*
Sheba: Queen Makeda's Rule. *19*

Chapter Three
The Development of the Caste System and
the Aryan Conquest 25
Beliefs and Migration of the Aryans *26*

Chapter Four

Ahab, Ahaz, and Hezekiah's Reigns
in Israel and Judah..46
   The Reign of King Ahab and
the Conflict with Elijah 47
   Ahaz's Reign and the Fall of Israel..................................... 50
   Hezekiah's Resistance to Assyria and
Manasseh's Wicked Reign 53

Chapter Five

The Conquest of Babylon and the Tragic Fate
of Kings 61
   The Fall of Nineveh and the Babylonian Revolt 61
   Judah's Future Prophecies and Warnings 63

Chapter Six

Dreams, Madness, and Redemption in the Life of King
Nebuchadnezzar 81
   Greece: From the Ancient Hellenes to Alexander the Great...... 90

Chapter Seven

Ancient Rome and Carthage Heroes and
Tragedies 100
   The Destruction of Carthage and t
he Third Punic War 101
   The Life and Teachings of Jesus Christ
in Palestine... 107

Chapter Eight

From Biblical Curses to Imperial Exploitation:
The African and American Saga..117
   The Devastating Consequences of European Colonization..... 118
   British Rule to American Freedom.. 132

Chapter Nine

The Abolitionist Movement: Battling Slavery and Racial
Inequality...142

The Struggle for Education and Liberation *150*
The Road to Emancipation and the Abolition
of Slavery *155*

Chapter Ten

The American Civil War: Division, Emancipation, and the
Transformation of a Nation.......................................159

Civil Rights Struggles, Sacrifice, and Equality..................... *171*

Chapter Eleven

The Historical Narratives of Rwanda, Burundi,
and South Africa in the Eyes of Ezekiel...............176

Divine Judgments and Prophetic Warnings.......................... *181*
Isaiah and Revelation's Visions of Restoration
and Judgment *188*
Conversion of Paul, Idolatry Warning,
and Spiritual Warfare *194*

Chapter Twelve

The Final Call: America's Caste System and the Quest for
Liberation..199

God's Judgment and the Youthful Nation *206*

Conclusion *228*

Bibliography *230*

Acknowledgment

This book, "CUSH To MYSTERIOUS BABYLON: Africa and the Covenant People," honors the courageous and visionary individuals who have resisted racism, oppression, unfairness, and injustice. It also recognizes those who have inadvertently compromised the freedoms and well-being of others to uphold the status quo. First and foremost, I want to thank the unidentified people who have dedicated their lives to combating bigotry and prejudice. Your commitment to justice and equality inspires us. This book recognizes your trials, tribulations, and sacrifices. I'd want to thank everyone who shared their stories, thoughts, and experiences. Your willingness to address societal issues is critical. I will be forever grateful to your voices for bringing my narrative to life.

My family was supportive of me when I was writing this book. It would not have been possible without your help, patience, and understanding. I'm fortunate to have such wonderful support. I also want to thank the countless scholars, historians, lecturers, and activists who have helped us understand racism and injustice throughout history and in the present. Your efforts have made the globe a more welcoming and fairer place. I'm thankful to everyone, both visible and unseen, who assisted with this project. This book recognizes the African Covenant People and those who strive for equality.

I appreciate it,

Michael Ray Lemons.

Introduction

It is perplexing how skin shades influence various aspects of human behavior, from racial issues to political fate, the judicial system, and economic status. Claiming our nation's history and current tendencies toward oppression, inequality, and injustice are unrelated to race or skin tone would be dishonest. The caste system's hierarchy subtly contributes to human division, adding an underlying sense of sorrow to our social interactions. This system prevents an equilibrium or a state of physical stability within humanity. It further shows that originating from immigrant settlers from the Balkans, the caste system has spread its supremacy to India, Egypt, the Aegean Islands (Greece and Rome), and throughout the Western world as a paradigmatic structure.

Determining one's position on the socioeconomic ladder involves philosophical questions regarding racial stereotypes. Although we are all children of God, our egos sometimes take precedence, acting as badges of honor. Many individuals wrestle with this mindset, either elevating others to higher social positions or casting negative shadows upon those with a lower societal status. Discrimination against individuals with varying skin tones or perceived economic statuses continues to persist. A troubling phenomenon exists whereby differences in skin color, religion, or wealth can provoke hostility and transform ordinary people into aggressors. It is crucial for everyone to actively dismantle the barriers created by prejudice, injustice, and systemic racism.

CHAPTER ONE

Skin Colors:
From Historical Oppression to
Global Power Structures

In the early years (1904-1907), the Germans slaughtered over 60,000 Herero people and an unknown number of San and Nam populations in what is now Namibia, located in southwest Africa. This event marked the first state-sponsored ethnic killings of the twentieth century and laid the foundation for the term "genocide," derived from the Greek word "genos" and the Latin word "cide" (killing). This genocide was a precursor to numerous other mass killings rooted in the racial hierarchy that rationalized such a holocaust. Baskets filled with skulls and the remains of massacred tribespeople were transported to Germany as evidence of racial supremacy. The perpetrators wore their heinous acts like a badge of honor, devoid of the empathy needed to recognize their victims as fellow human beings.

European Genocide in Namibia and Congo

In 2004, the German government acknowledged the genocide to the United Nations High Commissioner for Human Rights but did not offer financial compensation to the victims' descendants or a formal apology. The Germans had adopted a deeply ingrained belief in the superiority of the Aryan race and considered all other members of the human family to be inferior. This belief relegated people of African descent to outcast status and positioned them at the lowest rung of the social hierarchy.

Some scholars argue that the brutality in Central Africa, particularly under King Leopold of Belgium's rule in the Congo Free State (now the Democratic Republic of the Congo), epitomizes one of history's most horrifying genocides.

During this time, widespread atrocities and violence occurred, and the Congolese population significantly declined. The cycle of violence in Africa manifested as a seemingly endless pattern of ruthless brutality. Across the continent, the tale repeated itself, with Congo being a prime example. Under King Leopold's rule, all land - whether farmland or residential areas - and any natural resources found above or below ground, were his direct property.

Between 1885 and 1908, Leopold II designated the Congo Basin as a private charity. Under his rule, the Congolese were subjected to forced labor, and coerced into harvesting rubber and other precious resources. Leopold did not hesitate to annihilate entire communities to fulfill his demands. When targets fell short, unspeakable violence ensued – countless innocent lives were decapitated, their severed body parts gruesomely displayed on towering skull racks. These haunting scenes marched through the streets, culminating in the incineration of the remains. This dark era killed an estimated 10 to 15 million Congolese souls.

It's difficult to fathom how numerous wars were deeply rooted in seizing others' possessions for financial and political gains. Despite the warm embrace of Africans toward Europeans, they were met with oppression in return. The schemes of imperialism and exploitation lay beneath the façade of smiles and refuge requests.

The British Commonwealth and Nazi Germany engaged in monumental clashes in North Africa and the East African Desert Campaign, resulting in the senseless massacre of countless innocents. This heinous violence ignited a collective call to action, propelling the United States to enter the fray because of relentless civilian butchery. Officially joining the war in December 1941, Africans were once again compelled to serve their colonial rulers, as they had previously done during the First World War.

The First World War revealed the powerful impact of psychological warfare through media, disseminating disturbing accounts of gruesome mutilations, relentless rape cycles, and the indiscriminate slaughter of innocent civilians. Propaganda emerged as a powerful weapon while countless lives were lost based on race, ethnicity, or religion. After the Second World War, Germany was compelled to relinquish its colonies to the Allies. Both World Wars profoundly altered the way Africans perceived themselves. The focus on European economic progress shifted towards a mounting desire for liberty. African leaders recognized that maintaining colonies could plunge European powers into civil unrest and mayhem.

Post-WWII Changes and Independence Struggles

After the Second World War, Africa seemed virtually invisible globally. The continent faced ongoing internal upheavals and radical regime changes as it transitioned from colonial rule to independent states. European companies spearheaded efforts to exploit mining profits for shareholders through economic subterfuge rather than genuinely aiding African nations in their quest for decolonization. As the British Empire crumbled, new opportunities arose for Africans and reshaped European countries seeking to flourish independently.

The Second World War ushered in a renewed sense of political freedom and autonomy for Africa. On March 6, 1957, Ghana - formerly known as the Gold Coast - became the first Sub-Saharan African nation to achieve independence.

The dream of economic prosperity shone brightly for young Africans, yet some European leaders advocated the divisive strategy of divide and conquered to hinder its growth. These leaders fiercely resisted the notion of Black Africans governing states throughout the continent.

The Second World War acted as an economic catalyst for South Africa, elevating the value of platinum, uranium, and steel. However, Black Africans were excluded from this economic boom and stripped of their freedom. As a result, a fierce fight for liberty unfolded, with protests igniting the nation like steam released from a pressure cooker.

In 1943, the United National Party triumphed in the general election and adopted a chillingly pro-white stance. This party had long been proponents of apartheid and white supremacy policies, ultimately crafting a statement introducing apartheid (the Afrikaans term for "separateness") to describe their discriminatory segregation program.

The British Commonwealth vehemently opposed the white-majority rule government for implementing apartheid policies, ultimately forcing South Africa to renounce its ties to the British monarchy and exit the Commonwealth. As a result, South Africa transitioned into an independent republic, upholding its racial segregation policies.

In Rwanda, the Belgian League of Nations instituted a compulsory ethnic identity card system, categorizing individuals as Hutu or Tutsi. Researchers from the United States and Europe were sent to examine skull and brain measurements, and their findings were misused, asserting that Tutsis had a lighter skin tone. Consequently, the Belgians gave the Tutsis political control despite the Hutu majority.

When the European league withdrew from Rwanda, massive violence erupted, leading to more than a million deaths as global onlookers remained passive. Despite having forces stationed in Rwanda by the United Nations and Belgium and a US embassy, no one received authorization to end these brutal massacres.

The tragic situation began to shift only when rebels led by Paul Kagame initiated attacks from Uganda and waged a guerrilla-style campaign against the Hutu-dominated Rwandan Army. Paul Kagame and his Rwandan Patriotic Front (RPF) battled against the Congolese Army, which sided with the Hutus.

Paul Kagame and his rebel forces swept through the Democratic Republic of Congo's capital, Kinshasa, overthrowing the government and establishing Laurent Kabila as president. During this upheaval, Sub-Saharan Africa - from the Congo to the ancient world of the Aegean Islands - found itself at war with Eurocentric ideals.

The African continent had already witnessed numerous invasions before merciless conquerors arrived in the name of a God, they barely understood themselves. Like a swarm of locusts, missionaries descended upon Africa, disrupting its cultural and social foundations. Gradually, these missionaries made way for soldiers who aimed to seize land and plunder its riches.

The challenge of connecting the experiences of African people forcibly taken from their homeland via the Middle Passage (the infamous route across the Atlantic) to those who remained on the continent became a focal point in Black literature. The transatlantic slave trade marred the crucial contributions of early African civilizations and stunted their economic growth. Undoubtedly, Africa's abundant resources, ranging from food to gold and precious stones, captured European explorers' attention and fueled their insatiable greed.

Despite the undeniable reality, society chose to overlook the emotional torment suffered by Africans as they were shackled side by side aboard slave ships. With stops at various destinations, the agony of enslavement remained constant, be it in Europe or anywhere in the Americas. The African diaspora residing in the New World, alongside most of those on the African continent, had to endure life under oppressive rulers. Negative stereotypes were perpetuated to rationalize this mistreatment.

The strategy of white supremacy sought to influence the narrative and enact laws prohibiting Africans, particularly those in the New World, from learning knowledge or prospering from their labor. This situation shaped the experience of Black Africans and influenced the development of Black communities in the New World. In a twisted and vicious manner, the abuse inflicted upon Black and brown individuals advanced white society in Europe and the United States. Africa's existence and its magnificence became less significant to Eurocentric thinkers, who continued propagating derogatory portrayals of Black Africans as inferior to Anglo-Saxon whites.

The caste system and white privilege persisted on an ominous trajectory, resembling a rapidly spreading virus. The

Nazi regime clung to age-old notions of pure Aryan bloodlines as they dismantled the Black power structure through genocide. Hitler's warped convictions led him to single out Jews as bearers of concealed African DNA.

Meanwhile, Western Europe and the United States adopted a more contemporary approach to oppressing Black and brown people, further fueling capitalism.

This strategy helped enable industrial growth and financial capital to thrive, leading Western Europe and the United States of America to expand into global economic power structures rapidly.

CHAPTER TWO

Cush: The Legacy and Impact of Africa's Oldest Civilization

Similar to earlier historical names on the Genesis' ethnological table, the term "Cush" (also spelled Kush) can refer to an ethnicity and an individual. Moreover, it serves as a geographical reference for identifying nations and tribes. In the Hebrew Bible, Cush was used to denote the son of Ham and the name assigned to the tribal region inhabited by his descendants. The Kingdom of Cush referred not only to the geographic area corresponding to present-day Ethiopia but also broadly encompassed dark-skinned people residing along the Nile in southern Egypt, Sudan, Eritrea, Somalia, and beyond India's borders.

The Book of Genesis provides an insightful ethnographic account that traces the descendants of Cush through the Table of Nations. The ancient nation of Cush (also known as ancient Ethiopia) holds a prominent position in biblical scriptures as one of the first nations mentioned and potentially the cradle of civilization on earth. Many scholars widely acknowledge the African continent as humanity's birthplace.

During ancient times, numerous Cushitic individuals migrated to fertile regions along vital rivers such as the Nile, Sahara, Tigris, and Euphrates. The land they inhabited became known to Greeks as Ethiopia - translated as "burned face" - owing to early European explorers' belief that residents had been scorched by intense sunlight.

Cush's and the Kushites' Legacies

Cush, as the first-born son of Ham and the grandson of Noah, holds an important place in history. His son Nimrod migrated to Shinar, where he constructed prominent cities such as Babel, Nineveh, Calneh, Erech, and Accad. The Old Testament's reference to the land of Cush near the Garden of Eden utopia makes these events more intriguing. The Genesis creation story provides a backdrop for exploring this connection further, as it describes the four rivers of paradise that flow in the vicinity.

> [10]*Now a river went out of Eden to water the Garden, and from there it parted and became four riverheads.* [11]*The name of the first is Pishon; it is the one which skirts the whole land of Havilah, where there is gold.* [12]*And the gold of the land is good. Bdellium and onyx stone are there.* [13]*The name of the second river is Gihon; it is the one which goes around the whole land of Kush.* [14]*The name of the third river is Hidekel; it is the one which goes toward the east of Assyria. The fourth river is the Euphrates.*
>
> *(New King James Version, Genesis 2:10-14).*

The Cushites, ancestors of modern-day Ethiopia, hold the title of the oldest African nation. Enthusiasts of Afrocentric literature celebrated their discovery that most Cushitic languages stem from ancient Ethiopia. A significant moment occurred in 1974 when "Lucy," the oldest human fossil, was discovered in Ethiopia's Afar Triangle. This find shifted perspectives to Africa being the cradle of human existence.

Cush, a region in Sub-Saharan Africa, boasts an array of historical sites, including thousands of pyramids established during the ancient Kingdom of Cush. The Great Pyramid of Giza, located on Cairo's outskirts, is the largest and oldest remaining wonder from the Seven Wonders of the Ancient World. This iconic tomb housed the dynasty Pharaoh Akhet Khufu and his family during the thriving Kushite kingdom.

Once considered the tallest artificial structures globally, some speculate that extraterrestrial life forms created these massive pyramids. Alternatively, it could simply be evidence that the Afrocentric people from this era possessed greater intelligence than we give them credit for today. Imhotep, the peacemaker, was a remarkable figure in ancient Egypt who constructed the impressive Pyramid of Djoser in Saqqara. As a genius in architecture, medicine, sculpting, writing, and astronomy, he was a trusted advisor during the Pharaoh's third dynasty.

Together with King Djoser, Imhotep developed an innovative tomb called the mastaba to shield noble and royal graves from wild creatures. They dug the foundation into the earth's bedrock and adorned it with stones. Masonry sand filled the base while carefully arranged limestone blocks were piled on top. A labor force of workers and enslaved people placed these bulky stones on rollers or sleds and masterfully aligned them.

The pyramid was strategically located to catch the sunlight as it streamed from above. As a groundbreaking monument of its time, the Pyramid of Djoser hosted beautifully crafted chapels near its base alongside funeral temples and a grand courtyard reserved for royalty. Mastabas were continuously stacked layer upon layer, with an outer wall coated in sleek white limestone finished with steps or a staircase. Eventually, this led to the creation of the world's very first pyramid.

The walls inside the pyramid showcased intricate hieroglyphics that depicted various scenes such as victorious battles, wildlife, vegetation, birds, and everyday activities like hunting, fishing, and farming. These stunning carvings often featured the king alongside his esteemed subjects. Even after nearly 5,000 years, this elegant engraving maintains its breathtaking artistry. It is a testament to ancient Egypt's prowess in building structures and artwork that endure longer than any other civilization on our planet. In Egypt, archaeologists uncovered a collection of ancient papyrus documents, believed to be the oldest in the region. These vital historical records reveal hieroglyphic images that offer a glimpse into the construction of pyramids and daily life along the Nile.

Egyptian hieroglyphics portray Kushites with darker skin, braids, and woolly hair, providing insights into their culture from the earliest Egyptian literature. Over time, Eurocentrism emerged and expanded around the Nile Delta and Mediterranean regions.

Egypt's once uninhabitable Nile Valley eventually saw small communities thriving along the riverbanks. Life here consisted of clearing land, constructing irrigation channels, and building dams near the delta where the Nile flows into the Mediterranean Sea.

The Nile River has long been a source of fascination for people worldwide. Flowing through 11 different African countries, it originates from the highlands of Ethiopia and Uganda's White Nile, making its way to Lake Victoria and beyond. This great river travels through mountain crevices in the Lake Albert region and winds through dense swamps, creating a complex network of water channels. As it rushes over waterfalls and races down the Rift Valley, the Nile nurtures plant life and grazing animals. In time, its seasonal flows deliver rich soil deposits to the thriving Nile Delta.

The allure of Aswan as a sacred and idyllic haven in Afrocentric beliefs is undeniable. Even before setting foot in Canaan (modern-day Israel), the Israelites could appreciate and contribute to Aswan's thriving city-state. The sacred nature of Aswan in Afrocentric views implies that it was considered the ultimate paradise on Earth. Aswan, the famed city on the Nile River, served as southern Egypt's strategic and commercial hub, with majestic cataracts to the north nourishing the land and fueling agricultural prosperity in Lower Egypt. The ancient Kushites played a vital role in Egypt's development, and it's clear that the Egyptians have a lot to thank the Cushitic people for. Sharing a common ancestry, the Cushites and Egyptians contributed to the spread of Afro-Asiatic culture throughout the Mediterranean.

Per the scriptures, there were no births in the Garden of Eden. All because Adam and Eve ate from the Tree of Knowledge and were banished from this paradise. Then came the firstborn status or the Covenant, taking center stage with humanity's first birth in Aswan. The Bible guides us to where this miracle happened, making Pathros (upper Aswan), now part of modern-day northern Sudan, the holiest place on Earth. While the Israelites' Covenant didn't replace Aswan's significance, it did help spread Yahweh's blessings and abundance. The Covenant can either be a divine gift or a source of spiritual weakness, leading to dreadful plagues.

The Cushitic people and the ancient Israelites share a common heritage and have always held great pride in their connection to Aswan - their ancestral homeland situated south of Egypt. This sacred land brought immense unity among the Afro-Asiatic population until the emergence of new religions from the Balkans. The introduction of these polytheistic beliefs ultimately caused division among the Egyptians, Israelites, and Cushites. Aswan is fascinating in the history of the Jewish people and ancient Ethiopians due to its connection with their firstborn status. Isaac's birth couldn't overshadow the importance of the ancient Aswan's firstborn covenant within the human family. As part of God's chosen people, the Children of Jacob had their unique connection to this covenant through Abraham, Isaac, and Jacob.

Interestingly, the original inhabitants of Cush were considered part of the Hebrew-speaking community, with various groups conversing in distinct Hebrew dialects. Some of these languages are thought to have vanished entirely. To fully understand the divide between the Cushites, Egyptians, and Israelites, one must explore the deep-rooted stigma that separates them. It's a shame how many Eurocentric writers have stripped the identity of the ancient Hebrews from the Indigenous African people, diminishing their significance in world history. What's fascinating is that all humans can trace their roots back to Africa's Cush region, pointing us towards a shared origin story. I will bring back captives of Egypt and cause them to return to the land of Pathros (upper Aswan), the land of their origin. (Ezekiel 29:14) Are you not like the people of Cushites to Me, O children of Israel? (Amos 9:7)

The Cushites formed vibrant communities that grew into bustling city-states, acting as hubs for governing power. These city-states came together to create the world's first magnificent civilization, lasting until around 350 A.D. Cush was a melting pot of ideas for the Ancient Ethiopian people, where they exchanged expertise in agriculture, art, farming, religion, mining, and metalwork. Pioneering bronze tools instead of stone, the Cushites became the first sophisticated society to trade with distant merchants like those in India. They established higher learning institutions and a long-lasting governance system that thrived for millennia.

Once upon a time, the Kingdom of Cush flourished in northern Sudan, with Meroe as its stunning capital. Sadly, Meroe fell to flames in the fourth century A.D., pushing the incredible Cushites to seek new horizons in northeast Africa, where the Aksumite Empire thrived.

The legend of the Cushite people still echoes today as they shaped our world with their extraordinary skills, profound literature, spiritual depth, and scientific innovation. No other civilization has quite sparkled like them. Even Greece and Rome took inspiration from their artistic brilliance.

At its zenith, Cush was a superstar in the ancient world; even the Egyptians could trace their roots back to these glorious ancestors. Remnants of their story live on within us, inviting us to explore and embrace their incredible legacy.

The Cushites were master farmers, hunters, ironworkers, and extraordinary builders. Their empire spread across the Mediterranean and the Aegean Islands, dominating their agricultural way of life. They grew various crops, such as wheat, barley, turnips, watermelon, corn, lettuce, onion, garlic, and materials for linen production.

The lush Nile Delta was home to the finest vineyards, producing figs, blackberries, strawberries, mulberries, and pomegranates. Grapes were plentiful and used to create wine for both entertainment and ceremonies. The Cushites also enjoyed hunting a wide range of wild birds and animals like lions, leopards, wildebeests, gazelle, oxen, warthogs, impala, sheep, and goats. Fishing spots were abundant—from mountain streams to ocean coastlines.

With an ideal food-growing climate, the Cushites recognized fabric-making as an ordinary female skill. Women played an essential role in society by crafting garments and spinning and weaving clothes for royalty. Their skillful hand's designed fashion added to the allure of their mighty empire that sprawled across three continents.

SATAN'S IMPACT AND PAGANISM

The Koran captures the complex dynamics between humanity and the head of the fallen angels in this captivating excerpt:

We created man from dry clay, from black molded loam, and before him Satan from smokeless fire, Your Lord said to the angels 'I am creating man from dry clay, from black molded loam… The angels, one and all, prostrated themselves except Satan. He refused to prostrate himself with the others. He replied, "I will not bow to a mortal whom You created of dry clay of black moulded loam."

"Be gone," said God, "you are accursed, my curse shall be on you until the Day of Judgment Day!"

(Koran AL-Hijr 15:25-41)

"Lord," said Satan, "since You have seduced me, I will tempt mankind on earth; I will seduce them all, except those of them who are your faithful servants."

He replied, "This is My straight path, you shall have no power over My servants, only the sinners who follow you."

I am nobler than he; he replied. You created me from fire, but You created him from clay. He said: Get down hence! This is no place for your contemptuous pride.

(Koran The Height 7:11)

When Satan fell from grace, he convinced a third of the angels to rebel against the Creator's rules. These banished angels remained unseen, but through magic, sorcery, and idol worship, people could control these ill-intentioned beings to harm their foes. The fallen angels had one goal: to lure humans away from God by granting supernatural powers and creating special bonds with those aligned with these spiritual entities.

Over time, this strong interaction with nature transformed into mythology. Pagan nations devoted themselves to their gods by crafting statues, images, and altars. The Balkan settlers, also known as Aryans, constructed temples in the most sacred locations for divination and honoring their chosen deities.

In the intriguing book of Isaiah, Lucifer's dramatic descent from grace is portrayed alongside the anticipated collapse of Babylon in the following passage:

> [12]*How you are fallen from heaven,*
> *O Lucifer, son of the morning!*
> *How you are cut down to the ground,*
> *You who weakened the nations!*
> [13]*For you have said in your heart:*
> [14]*I will ascend into the heaven,*
> *I will exalt my throne above the stars of God;*
> *I will also sit on the mount of the congregation on the farthest sides of*
> *the north;*
> *I will ascend above the heights of the clouds,*
> *I will be like the Most High.*
> [15]*Yet you will be brought down to Sheol,*
> *To the lowest depths of the Pit.*
>
> *(New King James Version, Isaiah 14:12-15)*

The rebellious angels were banished from heaven, yet they maintained some connection with the Creator as rogue accusers. In Job's story, Satan is powerless due to his unwavering faithfulness and devotion. Job's commitment is tested when a devastating combination of fire and wind wipes out his livestock. Despite this tragedy, he remains steadfast in praising God, and his wife scolds him for it:

> *¹Now there was a day when the sons of God came to present themselves before the Lord, and Satan also came among them. ²And the Lord said to Satan, "From where do you come?" So, Satan answered the Lord and said, "From going to and fro on the earth, and walking back and forth on it." ³Then the Lord said to Satan, "Have you considered My servant Job, that there is none like him on the earth, a blameless and upright man, one who fears God and shuns evil?"*
>
> *(New King James Version, Job 1:6-7)*

As the massive ice glaciers on Europe's steppes melted, settlers from the Balkans could finally interact with the rest of the world. However, this reunion also led to clashes of race, ethnicity, and religion. Satan exploits these differences to spread his beliefs and empower those he selects. `In sacred texts, Satan tempts people to worship him rather than God. As the Hindu Vedas mention, Aryan Gentiles accepted this offer to carry out the wishes of the gods (fallen angels), hoping to reinforce the caste hierarchy. Consequently, the Eurocentric value system rose against those with Afrocentric features. Over time, this caste system was passed down through strict Pagan customs, effectively making people of color second-class citizens.

In the Nile Delta, the Sea People from the Balkans, known as the Biblical Philistines, overthrew the covenant people and plunged them into chaos. This led to the rapid spread of paganism throughout the Israelite and Cushite lands. The influence of these new pagan practices spread rapidly in every direction, like an unstoppable wildfire.

For a long time, the Aryans lived in the mountainous region of the Balkans during the Stone Age. They relied on tools made from bones and rocks for everyday tasks, combat, and hunting. Meanwhile, civilizations near the Nile, Euphrates, and Tigris rivers were already using metals and learning how to farm and raise livestock. As glaciers retreated due to climate change, the Aryans discovered an advanced Negroid civilization that used silver and gold utensils for eating and built intricate structures with artistic murals on their walls.

Long ago, the mighty Nile River would burst its banks every year from June to September, all thanks to monsoon rains in the Ethiopian Highlands. The Egyptians named the lush, green valley nourished by the Nile the "Black Land" due to its dark soil deposits, while they called the surrounding desert the "Red Land." However, whenever the river swelled too much, its powerful currents wreaked havoc on everything in their way. The Nile gracefully meandered along Egypt and served as the backbone of Cushite region. As Earth's longest river, it winds through East Africa's mountains and eventually flows northwards through the Sahara Desert before spilling into the Mediterranean Sea. Geologists have discovered evidence that the Cushites built a thriving civilization along these bountiful waters.

In the region's welcoming climate, fertile lands invited farming, grazing, and mining, showering the area with priceless jewels, ivory, and gold. Cushites created lovely attire and pottery while constructing luxurious buildings through ingenious methods. The Nile Valley's nutrient-rich earth served as some of the most prosperous farmland in ancient times, with Lower

Egypt flourishing from the soil delivered by the Nile River from Ethiopia. Learning to construct earthen dams, Egyptians harnessed the river's power and thrived thanks to Ethiopia's highlands.

As settlers journeyed further, they formed villages and city-states. Over time, they designed irrigation systems for self-sustainability and to support larger populations. They became proficient in carpentry, masonry, weaving, and pottery while building protective walls around their cities against potential threats.

Long ago, the Sahara was a lush oasis filled with lakes and streams. Today, it's a vast desert stretching across an area nearly as large as the United States. The ancient Cushites settled around the Sahara and the Mediterranean, bringing their rich culture and farming techniques. They tamed animals and practiced agriculture before spreading across the Afro-Asiatic region. Back then, the Sahara was a thriving land with grasslands, forests, and wetlands where they cultivated crops like rice, yams, wheat, barley, and more. Over time, the climate became drier, transforming the area into a desert. This forced many people to migrate southward, spreading across the Sahara toward the Red Sea, Egypt, and Africa.

SHEBA: QUEEN MAKEDA'S RULE.

Once upon a time, in a mountainous region in southwestern Arabia along the Red Sea's eastern shore, there was a mystical land called the Kingdom of Sheba. The legendary Queen of Sheba, known as Queen Makeda, ruled these lands with grace and power. This realm's existence can be traced back to Saba, the eldest son of Cush and grandson of Ham, as mentioned in the ancient book of Genesis. Nestled along the Nile River, the kingdom's vibrant capital city - also named Saba - flourished with abundant lush crops. These bounties spread across Ethiopia, enriching the entire region. Interestingly, Sheba was not only a place but also the name of Cush's grandson. It is inferred in the New Testament that Sheba represents the prophetic Queen of the South who will rise again in the latter days and stretch her hand toward God with enthusiasm and devotion.

In the New Testament's book of Galatians, Apostle Paul shares his incredible conversion experience with Jesus Christ (or Yeshua Ha'Mashiach in Hebrew) and how it led him to Arabia (Sabean) on his first missionary journey. Sabean, a part of the lush Cushite lands, was well-known for its profitable trade opportunities. This bountiful region produced valuable frankincense and myrrh from the trees growing along its mountainsides and coast. The Great Dam of Marib (Wadi Dhana) served as a primary water supply, further adding to its allure.

The dam was an intricate network of canals and storage tanks ingeniously designed to gather rainwater for irrigation using earthen barriers. Massive stones were used to build the waterway, channeling river, and rainwater through tunnels and sluices toward homes and public spaces. The aqueducts supplied water for the mountain's lush botanical gardens and created a well-thought-out distribution system around cities that stood the test of time. Cleverly, the Sabeans built the dam to capitalize on heavy flooding during the monsoon season, from June to November. Monsoon winds were navigation aids since they carried travelers toward India and the Far East before changing direction.

The Sabeans were expert traders, dealing in grains, fruits, precious metals, and various spices. Their trade network was extensive, utilizing camel caravans across Africa and sailing to distant India. They held a monopoly over regional trade routes alongside their neighbors. Their homeland was naturally protected by its unique geography, including mountains, a massive dam, and the mighty Nile River, which made invasions difficult on enemies. One such encounter occurred during Augustus Caesar's rule when the Sabeans clashed with Roman forces over Syene. Ultimately, the Sabeans emerged victorious, driving the Romans into the desert, where many perished to thirst. As a trophy of this triumph, they seized a bronze head statue of Emperor Augustus Caesar.

The Bible and Koran's religious teachings warned the Sabeans against worshiping Pagan gods, as this would distance them from the Lord's unwavering protection and leave them feeling insecure and vulnerable. The initial covenant included the Israelites and the Sabeans (part of the Cushite community), who once resided under the Firstborn Covenant in present-day Arabia.

These ancient Ethiopians were expected to remain loyal to the Covenant, just like the Israelites, or face judgment if they strayed from obedience. The Cushites and Israelites shared a unique bond with a powerful, wise, and omnipresent God who sought their unwavering devotion. Their security and stability hinged on honoring and praising the Almighty God, Yahweh.

To uphold the Covenant, they had to follow the words of the prophets; otherwise, they risked provoking God's wrath, losing life-sustaining rain, and enduring plagues. Furthermore, it also meant possibly empowering their enemies to rise against them.

For the natives of Sheba, there was a sign in their dwelling; a garden on their right and a garden on their left we said to them, "eat of what your lord has given you and render thanks to Him. Pleasant is your land and forgiving is your Lord."

> *But they gave no heed. So, we let loose upon them the waters of the dam and replaced their gardens by two others bearing bitter fruits tamarisks and a few nettle shrubs. Thus, did we punish them for their ingratitude?*
>
> *(Koran Sheba 24:15)*

The waters will fail from the sea, and the river will be wasted and dried up. The river will turn foil. Thorns and briers will come on the land of My people (Isaiah 19:5). The enigmatic Queen of Sheba, also known as Queen Makeda, hailed from the Sabean region. While it remains unclear if she ruled over the entire Kingdom of Cush or just a portion of it, it's worth noting that Cush had lost some areas along the Nile, including Egypt, to the Aryans before her reign. These invaders demolished Cushite strongholds near the Nile, forcing the kingdom to retreat further south.

It's said that the captivating Queen of Sheba had her royal residence in Meroe, the capital of Cush. The renowned Jewish historian Josephus claimed that during her time, Sheba was not only queen of a united Cush but also Saba—the ancient island of Meroe—surrounded by the magnificent Nile and its tributaries, the Astapus and Astabaras rivers. This unique location further cemented her legendary status in history.

In the Koran, the curious queen embarked on a journey to test King Solomon's wisdom. A loyal Hoopie bird, Solomon's messenger, informed him about the captivating Kingdom of Sheba (Sabean). The Sabeans, mesmerized by celestial beings, had built a sacred temple in honor of Ilumquh (Sin) - the mesmerizing deity of the moon, Venus, and the sun. Undeterred, Solomon embarked on a mission to steer the queen and her people away from their enchanting pagan ways.

The bird, who was not long in coming, said: "I have just seen what you know nothing of. With truthful news I come to you from Sheba, where I found a woman reigning over a people. She is possessed of every virtue and has a splendid throne. I found that she and her subjects worship the sun instead of God. Satan has seduced them and debarred them from the right path, so that they might not be guided to the worship of God, who brings to light all that concealed in the heavens and the earth and knows what you hide and what you reveal God; there is no god but Him, the Lord of the Glorious Throne!"

(The Ant 27:22)

The enigmatic tale of Ethiopia's Sabean people captivates the imagination as their journey of faith in Yahweh, the one true God, weaves through their rise and fall. The Cushites, Egyptians, and Israelites hold strong ties to this magnificent civilization and even share their ancient Hebrew tongue.

But then, a dramatic twist occurred as their northern neighbors brought Pagan beliefs into the mix. The Sabeans, swept up in these newfound deities, saw their once-solid alliance fall apart. Interestingly, the Holy Bible considers the Cushites as God's firstborn children, and Isaiah 45:14 reveals the shared roots of Cush, Egypt, and the Sabeans. This verse even alludes to the Israelites being descendants of the Cushites!

Ask Me of things to come concerning My Sons; and the work of My hands. The Labor of Egypt and merchandise of Cush and the Sabeans, men of stature, shall come over in chains; and they shall bow down to you. (Isaiah 45:14)

Are ye not as children of the Cushites unto me, O children of Israel? saith the LORD {Amos 9:7)

[6]Because you have set your heart as the heart of a god, [7]Behold, therefore, I will bring strangers against you, the most terrible of the nations; and

they shall draw their swords against the beauty of your wisdom, and defile your splendor. ⁸They shall throw you down into the Pit, and you shall die the death of the slain in the midst of the seas.

(New King James Version, Ezekiel 28:6-8*)*

CHAPTER THREE

The Development of the Caste System and the Aryan Conquest

The Aryans were a fascinating and adventurous group who lived in the Ganges Valley and the Caucasus Mountains. They began their journey in Babylon and, after many generations, returned with fierce determination. These strong, long-haired individuals with light skin and European features were untamed and free-spirited. They traveled along the Oxus River, Jaxartes, Black Sea, and the Caspian Sea for centuries before finally reaching India. Another group of Aryans headed towards the Middle East and ancient regions like Persia, Assyria, Egypt, and Canaan before they became known as Hyksos. As brave warriors always in search of a home, the Aryans worshiped a multitude of gods in a sophisticated belief system focused on natural forces for divine blessings. They also recognized numerous other divine beings.

BELIEFS AND MIGRATION OF THE ARYANS

The Aryans practiced rituals and worshipped various gods connected to four unique realms: Earth, the underworld, the air in between, and lower heavenly realms. Building relationships with local gods, they integrated spirituality into their daily lives, constantly striving to please their chosen deities. They formed a social hierarchy known as Varna, meaning class or color. Convinced of their superior bloodline and divine authority, the Aryans felt a moral duty to govern all humankind. Known as Aryans or "Arya," they were also referenced in the Bible as Gentiles. This Aryan Gentile legacy passed on traits like pride, arrogance, and boldness that would eventually resonate globally.

The Aryans considered themselves elite, boasting remarkable intellect and destined to rule the world. They found a haven in India where devotion to Yahweh, the one true God, was rare except among a few tribal unions. The caste system they introduced forbade interracial marriages and showed little regard for other cultures. This sinister system of worship soon spread across the globe as the Aryans conquered new territories. Tracing their lineage to numerous civilizations, the Aryans became the forefathers of the Assyro-Babylonians, Dutch, Germans, Greeks, Persians, Portuguese, Spanish, French, Russians, Romans, and British. Daniel's Four Beast System arose from Aryan roots and the caste was once adopted by all gentile kingdoms as a divine representation of their governing structures.

Around 1800 BC., an enthralling battle occurred when the Aryans fought against India's dark-skinned inhabitants to take over their territories and resources. These native people, known as Shudra, Dasa, and Dravidians, fiercely defended their land. They shared many similarities with the Cushite people, making their history even more fascinating. These natives constructed fortified cities with houses crafted from baked clay bricks and lived vibrant lives. The Aryans described them as dark-skinned and thick-lipped folks who owned livestock and spoke an unfamiliar language. Determined to conquer, the Aryans navigated treacherous mountain paths using horse-drawn chariots and sophisticated weapons. Eventually, they overcame the Shudra fortifications, creating chaos and destruction throughout these lands in their ruthless conquest.

The Aryans were masters of battle, zipping around in their speedy chariots and striking from afar with their trusty bows. Armed with slings, sheaths, spears, and double-edged swords, they engaged in thrilling close combat. War was interwoven into their culture as they charged fearlessly on horseback or aboard lightning-fast chariots.

In a horrifying and swift attack, the Aryans swept across the land, marking one of the darkest massacres in human history. They took control of the territory and established themselves as rulers, expanding into new areas and decimating everything in their path. Originally nomadic hunters, the Aryans had no experience farming or raising animals like the native people they conquered.

However, as they claimed more land and power, they evolved from wandering tribes to rulers under a caste system. Realizing they needed workers for their new territories, the Aryans enslaved their captives rather than killing them. As they continued their conquests, the Aryans faced a powerful group of dark-skinned people called the Panis. Despite never entirely subduing them, the Aryans gradually wore down the Panis' resistance. The natives used mountainous terrain to hide and launch attacks to deny the invading force essential resources like food. Over time, however, Aryan customs began to spread and take hold, as even those who opposed them adopted their ways.

As the Shudra and Dasa tribes faced increasing pressure, many were forced into slavery or retreated deeper into the forest. They chose to distance themselves from the encroaching white settlers, relinquishing any hope of maintaining their freedom to wander the occupied lands. They lived like outlaws, fleeing from a relentless force commanded by the newly arrived white rulers. In the sacred Vedas, the Panis challenged the Aryans to break free from their devotion to pagan gods. They urged them to remember their shared ancestry and true beliefs.

(Panis) We have hidden the treasure in a place that is surrounded by mountains. There are cows, horses and many other riches...we know that you have been frightened by the gods and forced to come here. We look upon you as our own sister. Do not return to Indra. O beautiful one! Stay here. We will give you a share of the cows.

(Aryans) I cannot be your sister and you are not my brothers. I do not know these relationships. I only know Indra and the powerful Angirasa. When I return and tell Indra what has happened, he will come and invade you...O Panis flee away.

(Debroy, 1994)

The Aryans developed an intriguing caste system within the Hindu Varna, creating a well-defined social hierarchy to prevent interracial marriages. This system kept the darker-skinned population uninformed and excluded from religious ceremonies, preserving Aryan dominance. Crossing caste lines was strictly off-limits. The Aryans established a rigid system wherein each tribe was led by a chief who commanded a personal army for security. On top of that, they employed numerous priests to seek divine guidance, believing in the gods' powerful influence over human lives.

In ancient Aryan society, justice was served by mysterious forces that often-favored cruel intentions over fairness. The

Varna system determined People's social status from birth to death, dividing individuals based on their skin color. This caste system offered no fairness, as those in lower castes suffered immense hardships or faced horrific punishments, such as being skinned alive.

The brutal treatment of the Shudras, Dasa, and Dravidians makes this era one of the darkest times in human history. At the top of this hierarchy were the priests (Brahmins), who held significant power as they served as the gods' interpreters. They carried the gods' names and submitted themselves to higher-ranking members of Hindu society, thereby maintaining their influential position. In the intricate caste system of ancient India, the Kshatriya claimed the second spot, proudly showcasing their status as rulers and warriors. The Vaisyas came in third, a blend of Aryo-Dasa, embodying the essence of ordinary folks. Meanwhile, at the bottom was the Shudra – the enslaved people or peasants forced into servitude. Even lower than them, however, were the Untouchables – those with the darkest skin.

Think of it this way: the Shudra were ever-so-slightly elevated above the Untouchables but still scraping by just above ground level. As outcasts with dark complexions, they were deemed unworthy to be part of the caste-led social hierarchy. Remarkably, this caste system held sway over politics, economics, and religious life in India – an invisible puppeteer controlling society's every move.

In Hindu society, a hidden caste system determines one's social status from birth to death—the Aryan conqueror's associated dark skin with divine punishment. Shudras and Untouchables were at the bottom, forced into menial labor. This rigid hierarchy linked physical appearance to inherited privilege, influencing Hindu law and religious beliefs. The Indo-Europeans created the Aryan Bible, known as the Vedas, which consisted of four sacred texts: Rig-Veda, Yajur-Veda, Sama-Veda, and Atharva-Veda. These scriptures provided dedications, devotions, prayers, and hymns to the gods. Unsolicited exposure to Vedic teachings could lead to extreme punishments such as mutilation or death. They wanted to prevent those with higher melanin content from accessing these teachings. The Aryans prioritized adhering to their sacred rituals to appease the gods. For them, conducting religious rituals to please the gods was their top priority.

Countless gods and fallen angels demanded worship in the mystical world beyond our physical realm. Indra, the mighty god of thunder, storms, and war, held the highest significance during battles. The Aryans believed Indra could swoop in and protect them immediately, creating an unseen barrier between light and darkness. Indra was depicted as a fierce, vengeful deity with the power to unleash floods and fires upon his enemies. The ancient Hindu scripture, Rigveda, states that Indra despised the dark-skinned natives as they refused to bow down to the Aryan gods. In times of conflict, this god of thunder and war became more crucial than ever. Even today, India holds on to its deep-rooted connection with Indra by bearing his tribal name in their country's honour.

During special ceremonies, an empty seat was set aside on the grass near the fire for invisible guests. The guru, who acted as the altar-builder, prepared materials for the ritual and recited powerful mantras. They beckoned celestial beings to join in and enjoy the unique beverage made from the Soma plant, which had hallucinogenic properties. This drink was believed to help connect with spiritual presences.

Various rituals and festivals took place to understand better the divine forces of nature that connected everyone to hidden dimensions of reality. The Soma drink was mixed with water, milk, and honey before being placed on the grass near an evergreen tree. These trees symbolized life, wealth, and health and were honored by the Aryans due to their association with spiritual energy from the spirit world. They believed they could tap into more profound insights into the unseen forces shaping their lives by venerating these trees.

The evergreen tree held a magical aura, as people believed it communicated with celestial beings when the wind rustled its branches. They even thought it could summon lightning from the skies! These majestic trees became sacred spaces during spiritual ceremonies, where the ultimate offering was the sacrifice of newborn babies. This captivating tale has been shared for ages, capturing the essence of ancient beliefs and rituals. Through sacred ceremonies, the Aryans thanked Indra for defeating other spiritual beings, showing little to no mercy for the dark-skinned Natives. There are only three gods the Aryans of India made sacrificial offerings to: Agni, the fire god; Varuna, the god of the high-arched sky; and Indra, the god of storm and war, who controlled the weather, rain, thunder, and lightning. Agni represented all gods during the sacrifice and was believed to link humans to the divine world.

The Aryans' believed Brahma was a god more powerful and divine than the three gods to whom they made sacrifices. He was also more authoritative than all other gods. Brahma—not to be confused with the priest Brahmin—was all-powerful and all-knowing, the ultimate spiritual reality and the creator of all things, including all fallen and non-fallen angels. Brahma, the source of the entire world, emerged from the mysterious power of the One in Hinduism. He was connected to the eternal god of the Shudra, Dasas, and Panis, but for the Aryans, Brahma gradually lost his prominence on Earth and was no longer a central figure to be worshipped.

In "The Two Babylons," Reverend Alexander Hislop highlights a Vedic passage about Brahma's extraordinary greatness, stating no image can capture it. As the source of illumination and joy, all existence emanates from Brahma, life depends on him, and ultimately, everything returns to him.

The Greeks eventually categorized Brahma with the mysterious deities. Despite being the creator, Brahma received minimal devotion from the Aryan community. When the captivating Aryan faith from the Indus Valley combined with the others Euro-Aryans beliefs, a fascinating and complex religion was born, eventually evolving into what we now know as Hindu scriptures. Although both cultural groups had distinct names for their gods, their roles and belief systems were strikingly similar.

The caste system evolved into an elaborate mythology, but let's not forget - to the Aryans, these gods were real. They honored their divine idols through artistic depictions in statues and images.

The Aryan tribes ventured into the lush eastern region of the Middle East, nestled between the Tigris and Euphrates Rivers, eventually becoming the fierce Assyrians. They journeyed from the European highlands and headed toward the Mediterranean, growing increasingly ruthless and developing an eerie fascination with death. These warlike nomads displayed their gruesome trophies, beheading and skinning those they conquered before burning everything in their path. Assaulting cities, they buried their victims in pits, using their enemies' skulls as chilling goblets. Crafting clothing and cushions from their prey's skin, the merciless Assyrians aimed to strike fear into all who encountered them. They harbored a deep hatred towards dark-skinned natives and believed that divine forces favored the Aryan race.

The Assyrian Aryans were infamous for their ruthless massacres, tearing down buildings and scorching the earth. They took pride in their brutal conquests and sought material gain through prayer to their gods. When weakened, they made treaties, only to break them once their power was restored.

Ancient Egypt and Israel, and the Aryan Invasion

Once upon a time, a tribe of wandering Aryans shifted their focus to the land of Egypt. At that time, the region experienced little conflict from external forces. Three powerful kingdoms, Ethiopia, Nubia, and Egypt, were united under a single ruler in Memphis, forming the mighty Cushite Empire. The Egyptians did not need walls or immediate armies, as their neighbors shared the same culture and beliefs. The peoples of Egypt and Cush flourished together, mastering writing, math, and science. The Cushites were renowned for their advanced medical expertise - they could perform intricate surgeries on living patients. They pioneered groundbreaking techniques such as setting broken bones with casts and employing specialized physicians to address wounds and illnesses. Additionally, they were the first to develop mummification and embalming rituals for their deceased loved ones.

The famed historian Herodotus once observed the Ethiopians' fascinating embalming process, where they would coat their dearly departed with gypsum and skillfully paint the body to appear lifelike. The carefully preserved body was then placed in a crystal coffin that avoided unpleasant odors (Herodotus, 1982). The Ethiopians were also pioneers in art, sculpture, and architecture, creating awe-inspiring monuments and buildings. They cleverly engineered complex irrigation systems, dams, and bridges connecting vast land stretches. Ethiopians and Egyptians favored papyrus paper over other cultures' clay or animal skin for writing. Even their writing system was elaborate and artistic! They crafted hieroglyphics – a blend of engraved logographic and alphabetic elements – to curate religious literature with beauty and grace.

Among the fascinating achievements of the ancient Egyptians were their innovative ships and glass technologies. Their incredible educational advancements have captivated the human imagination throughout history. Despite their progress, a significant crisis struck Egypt when the Aryans invaded them. Priding themselves on their independence, the Egyptians faced nothing like this invasion before. Aryan warriors stormed in with advanced weapons and horse-drawn chariots, taking them by surprise. The Aryans pushed Egypt's borders down the Nile into Canaan (modern-day Israel), snatching territory from the Hittites, forever changing the course of Egyptian history.

Initially, Cushite leaders didn't dare confront the newcomers, known as the Hyksos. Instead, they acknowledged them as foreign rulers and maintained a truce. As innovative technologies transformed the region where the Aryans lived, the Hyksos' peaceful demeanor shifted dramatically. As their clan grew, they became more aggressive, wielding corporal punishment to squash even mild disobedience. The arrival of these Balkan settlers changed Egypt's reliance on Cush in many ways, mainly through enhancements to warfare. The Hyksos introduced horse-drawn chariots and composite bows, enabling swift attacks from long distances. This evolution marked the end of harmony between Cush and Egypt, dividing their lands forever.

The Hyksos launched a fierce attack on Upper Egypt, and forced the local inhabitants into slavery in Lower Egypt. As a result, Egyptians found themselves at the very bottom of the Eurocentric social hierarchy, living as enslaved people. The

Cush and Hyksos armies continued to battled it out to claim dominance over Egyptian lands. Hailing from a lower class of Balkan settlers, the Hyksos sought to claim their piece of wealth. They rallied their family clans with offers of free land and valuable treasures in Lower Egypt, resulting in a massive migration. This influx of newcomers tipped the balance in favor of the settlers, who became determined to seize territory and freedom from the Egyptians.

The new settlers journeyed to Canaan, now known as Israel and Palestine, and established five powerful kingdoms to control trade routes. They set up a hierarchy resembling that of the Indus Europeans in India, with the Pharaoh at its apex, considered a god on Earth. Nobles and priests encircled the pharaoh, performing daily rituals together. The Hyksos opted for a different approach - instead of massacring or enslaving the darker-skinned natives, they demanded submission to their higher status. The Aryans imposed their idol-based religion on the conquered people, tightly controlling the government and conscripting Egyptians into labor. They demolished old temples and erected new ones dedicated to their polytheistic gods. While invading, the Aryans enslaved Israelites and native Egyptians alike without distinction, as both had darker complexions.

The elite controlled the government and put the Egyptians to work. Many temples were demolished and replaced with new ones, honoring new polytheistic deities. Joseph found himself in Egypt's heart after his brothers sold him into slavery to Potiphar, a Pharaoh's court officer in Dothan (Genesis 37:17). Due to a severe drought in Canaan, Jacob and his family moved towards Egypt's southern border. Dothan, situated west of the Jordan River and northeast of Samaria, played a significant role. As Egypt's prime minister, Joseph allowed the Israelites to live in Goshen (Wadi Tumilat). Interestingly, there is no evidence that Aryans ruled Egypt during Joseph's life. He likely entered Egypt between 1900-1850 B.C., during Ethiopia's twelfth dynasty under the Ethiopian monarchy.

In the compelling book of Isaiah, the prophet intriguingly perceives the Hyksos and Assyrians as sharing a common cultural bond. Isaiah paints a vivid picture of the hardships faced by the Israelites during their captivity, as described in the following passage: "For thus says the Lord God..." My people went down at first into Egypt to dwell there; then, the Assyrians oppressed them without cause. Now therefore, what have I here," says the Lord, "That My people are taken away for nothing? Those who rule over them make them wail," says the Lord. (Isaiah 52:44-45)

Around 100 years after Joseph's demise, the Aryans likely invaded Egypt and ruled until the late 1500s. They were finally driven out during King Ahmose I's reign in the eighteenth dynasty. With the Cushites' assistance, Lower Egypt's natives rose, uniting with Upper Egypt to reclaim the Nile Delta. After overcoming Aryan oppression, they faced the Kushites, who sought control over the divided lands. This conflict persisted even when Moses appeared during the eighteenth dynasty. Called upon by the king to lead Egypt's army, a grown-up Moses led them to victory using his exceptional battle tactics and leadership skills. However, this success bred envy among the higher-ups who plotted against him.

Historian Josephus mentioned a war between Ethiopians and Egyptians during Thutmose's reign. Thutmose's military genius likely played a role in transforming Egypt into the world's first superpower. Afterward, an artistic revolution swept through Egypt with Minoan-inspired art arriving from migrating Cretans of the Aegean region. Following Amenhotep IV (Akhenaten)'s death, Prince Moses fled across the desert to Midian and eventually found favor among the Ethiopians. For a century after the Aryans were expelled, the Israelites continued to benefit from Joseph's influence. Despite kicking out the Aryans, the Egyptians adopted their governance, warfare strategies, and religious beliefs. They even embraced the Aryan caste system and forgot about the Creator God, Yahweh.

Rumors circulated that the Israelites were a chosen people with divine blessings. However, their humble lifestyle never showcased this extraordinary claim. They enjoyed support from a powerful Creator God who was so respected that divine beings from other realms would bow in His presence. The Israelites loved Egypt, a breathtaking paradise and the world's mightiest nation. Under the New Kingdom, Egyptians adopted many Aryan gods. Amun-Ra, the god of gods, became Egypt's primary deity. Numerous temples and pyramids were constructed across Nubia, enhancing Amun's worship. Military victories were attributed to Zeus-Amun's hidden influence. During their war campaigns, kings like Alexander the Great visited Amun's oracle near the Egyptian-Ethiopian border.

During the New Kingdom, Jacob's descendants lost their noble status as a new king took the throne in Egypt, unaware of Joseph's legacy (Exodus 1:8). These once privileged people were forced into harsh labor, with some working on tunnels for the tombs of ancient Egyptians. Constructing the magnificent temples required expert craftsmanship and an immense workforce. These structures displayed various scenes and texts that depicted everyday life and religious belief. The Israelites found themselves tasked with building storage cities and sacred temples for the pharaoh. They were responsible for creating mortar and bricks and working on construction projects. Additionally, they built levees and canals to protect cities from flooding caused by the rivers nearby.

In the book of Exodus, the Israelites built two prosperous cities for the pharaoh – Pithom and Raamses – near the Nile River (Ex. 1:11). As time passed, their workload grew heavier, and the pharaoh subjected them to great hardships. Fearing the fast expansion of the Israelite population, Pharaoh ordered the execution of all newborn male newborns. Fast forward 40 years, and Moses has been living in Midian. The king and those who wanted Moses dead were no more. One day, while tending his father-in-law Jethro's sheep, Moses noticed an astonishing sight on Mount Sinai – a bush on fire but not being consumed! As he approached to get a closer look, God called out to him from the burning bush.

> *4"Moses, Moses!" And Moses Answered, "Here I am." 5Then the Lord said, "Do not draw near this place. Take your sandals off your feet, for the place where you stand is holy ground. 6I am the God of your father- the God of Abraham, the God of Isaac, and the God of Jacob." Moses hid his face for fear of the Lord. 7The Lord said, "I have surely seen the oppression of My people who are in Egypt, and have heard their cry because of their taskmasters, for I know their sorrow.*
>
> *(New King James Version, Exodus 3:4-7)*

Moses bravely faced the new pharaoh, seeking permission to guide the Israelites to freedom. He returned to Egypt, echoing the Lord's powerful message: "Let My people go, that they may hold a feast to Me in the wilderness." The Pharaoh was unimpressed by Moses's requests, wondering, "Who is this Lord that I should follow His command to free Israel? I don't know of any Lord, and I'm not letting Israel go." As the seventh chapter begins, this unfolds:

At the beginning of the seventh chapter, it reads:

[1]See I have made you as God to Pharaoh and Aaron your brother shall be your prophet...[3]I will harden Pharaoh's heart, and multiply My signs and My wonders in the land of Egypt. [4]But pharaoh will not heed you, so that I may lay My hand on Egypt and bring My armies and My people, the children of Israel, out of the land of Egypt by great judgments.

(New King James Version, Exodus 7: 1-4)

Three months into their journey from Egypt, the Israelites found themselves at Mount Sinai, where the Lord appeared in a mysterious cloud and a pillar of fire. Blaring trumpets signaled His presence, and He reaffirmed the Covenant He'd created with Abraham, Isaac, and Jacob. This Covenant set the Israelites apart from other nations who practiced Paganism and idolatry. As they continued, Miriam and Aaron found fault with Moses for his marriage to an Ethiopian princess. They believed Moses broke tradition since Israelites were expected to marry within their tribes. But Moses had fallen in love with her while residing in Midian years before the Exodus. See how this ancient tale unfolds in the book of Numbers!

[10]"And the cloud departed from above the tabernacle suddenly Miriam became leprous, as white as snow. Then Aaron turned toward Miriam, and there she was, a leper. [11]So, Aaron said to Moses, "Oh, my lord! Please do not lay this sin on us, in which we have done foolishly and in which we have sinned."

(New King James Version, Numbers 12:10-11)

As the Israelites approached the edge of Edom, Moses reached out to Edom's king, seeking his blessing to cross the land. They set up camp in Kadesh, where Moses emphasized their shared heritage to win the king's favor.

14"Thus says your brother Israel: 'You know all the hardship that has befallen us, how our fathers went down to Egypt, and we dwelt in Egypt a long time, and the Egyptians afflicted us and our fathers."

(New King James Version, Numbers 20: 14)

When the king of Edom denied Moses' passage through his land, the Israelites had no choice but to change their path. Even though Moses saw the Edomites as brothers, their selfishness and jealousy created a division between them and the Israelites. As the Israelites journeyed on, they reached Acacia Grove near Moab. The king, unsettled by their presence, called upon Balaam to curse them. Moab's ruler, Balak, feared the Israelites would overrun their land after witnessing their victory against the Amorites. Consumed by worry, he believed they might exhaust all of their resources.

Balaam resided in Pethor, near the beautiful Euphrates River. The leaders of Moab and Midian sent royal envoys to Balaam, bearing gifts so he would curse the Israelites. However, the Lord told Balaam not to join them or curse the blessed people of Israel. So, Balaam asked the messengers to return home without him, as he lacked divine permission. Determined, Balak sent more envoys, presenting even more enticing rewards – piles of silver and gold! Now intrigued, Balaam met Balak at Moab's border and journeyed to Baal's high places atop Mount Peor. Hoping to impress Balak with sorcery, instead, Balaam found himself compelled by the Lord to utter prophetic blessings for the Israelites.

Balaam also revealed amazing prophecies about Israel's future triumphs over Edom and a mighty Messiah rising from Israel's lineage.

I see Him, but not now; I behold Him, but not near; A Star shall come out of Jacob; A Scepter shall rise out of Israel, batter the brow of Moab, and destroy all the sons of Tumult. And Edom shall be a possession; Seir also, his enemies, shall be a possession, while Israel does valiantly. Out of Jacob One shall have dominion, and destroy the remains of the city.

Before Balaam left, he informed the Moabite king about the Israelites' vulnerability and accepted the offered rewards. He let greed lead the Israelites astray, as mentioned in the Epistle of Jude: "Woe to them! For they have followed the path of Cain, pursued greed through Balaam's error for personal gain, and perished in Korah's rebellion" (Jude 1:11). The Israelites were then enticed to sacrifice and engage in Baal's worship, as well as commit immoral acts with Moabite and Midianite women, actions that infuriated the Lord.

The Philistines were the Israelites' deadliest foes. They'd sustained a naval defeat from the forces of Rameses III and had been driven further south into Syria and southern Canaan when the Iron Age began. Egyptian records indicate that the Philistines were the last group of Aryans to try to invade the 20th dynasty of Egypt during Rameses' thirty-one-year reign. In the seventh century B.C., the Assyrians, another sea people, rose to power under Esarhaddon's leadership and captured Egypt for world domination after marching into Memphis.

The Philistines' origins are shrouded in mystery, with only limited information in the Holy Bible. According to Genesis 10:14, they were sea people who descended from two tribal groups, Pathrusim and Casluhim, before settling in Caphtor, now known as Crete's coastal region. These aggressive seafarers searched for material possessions and often raided and burned towns and villages, bringing their deities of worship—Baal, Astarte, and Dagon—along with them. They first settled in three major cities in Canaan—Gaza, Ashkelon, and Ashdod—before pushing their way along the Mediterranean, Syria, and the southern coastal plains and central highlands of Canaan.

The Philistines were undoubtedly a force to be reckoned with, expanding into new territories like Gath and Ekron with impressive speed. Their economy was highly efficient, and they were known for their skillful tool-making and affinity for alcoholic beverages. With their advanced weaponry and chariots, they conquered the tribal territories of Dan and Judah, building a robust economy on the strength of their iron-fabrication expertise. Sadly, this was when the Israelites turned away from God, and the Philistines ruled with an iron fist. The Israelites depended on them for everything, including necessities like food and clothing. The Lord chose a devoted servant, Samson, as the final judge to guide the Israelites back to Him. During one memorable event, the Philistines sought vengeance on Samson for burning their crops by killing his wife and father-in-law. Samson had cleverly set their fields ablaze by tying lit torches to the tails of 300 foxes and releasing them among the Philistine lands.

Later, while Samson was smitten by a woman named Delilah, the Philistines found him in the Sorek Valley. They convinced Delilah to seduce Samson and uncover the secret behind his immense strength. In a moment of intoxication and laughter, Samson finally disclosed the source of his immense power: "A razor has never touched my head, as I have been devoted to God as a Nazirite since birth. If my hair is cut, I'll lose my strength, become weak, and be just like any other man" (Judges 16:17). As Samson slept, they chopped off his hair and summoned the Philistines to restrain him. The Philistines captured Samson, gouged out his eyes, and took him to Gaza. There, he was shackled in bronze chains and forced to grind grain. During a grand feast at the Temple of Dagon, the Philistine leaders gathered to offer sacrifices, unknowingly sealing their fate.

Samson was brought in to perform before a crowd of about 3,000 men and women, many of whom were on the rooftop, watching. After praying to the Lord for strength and remembrance, Samson exacted his revenge on the Philistines. He seized the supporting pillars of the Temple of Dagon and caused it to collapse, killing himself and the 3,000 Philistines present. The Israelites eventually triumphed over the Philistines by forming alliances with other Hebrew-speaking Cushite tribes. Among these Hebrew tribes were the Hittites, the largest group considered part of Canaan's inferior social class. They bravely fought alongside the Israelites, attacking Philistine towns and villages. These tribes discovered a shared purpose with the Israelites and united under the leadership of Samuel and King Saul. Together they declared, "If you return to the Lord with all your hearts, then put away the foreign gods and the Ashtoreth from among you, and serve Him only; and He will deliver you from the hand of the Philistines" (1 Samuel 7:3).

The Israelites chased down the Philistines, and amidst a roaring thunder, the Lord bewildered the Philistines, handed them over to the Israelites, and reclaimed the land. Throughout their lengthy journey from Egypt, the Lord cautioned the Israelites about the risks of adopting local traditions.

[24] Do not bow down before their gods or worship them or follow their practices. You must demolish them and break their sacred stones to pieces.

[25] Worship the LORD your God, and his blessing will be on your food and water. I will take away sickness from among you.

(New International Version, Exodus 23: 24-25)

Rather than driving out the Philistines, the Israelites embraced aspects of their culture, along with other Canaanite tribal traditions, without dismantling their spiritual centers. Additionally, the Covenant People faced religious differences with several non-Exodus Hebrew tribes who shared a common language but practiced the Canaanite faith.

[19] The LORD was with the men of Judah. They took possession of the hill country, but they were unable to drive the people from the plains, because they had chariots fitted with iron. [27] But Manasseh did not drive out the people of Beth Shan or Taanach or Dor or Ibleam or Megiddo and their surrounding settlements, for the Canaanites were determined to live in that land. [28] When Israel became strong, they pressed the Canaanites into forced labor but never drove them out completely.

(New International Version, Judges 1:19, 27, 28)

[1] The angel of the Lord went up from Gilgal to Bokim and said, "I brought you up from Egypt and led you to the land I promised to give your ancestors. I said, 'I will never break my agreement with you.

[2] But you must not make an agreement with the people who live in this land. You must destroy their altars.' But you did not obey me. How could you do this?

[3] Now I tell you, 'I will not force out the people in this land. They will be your enemies, and their gods will be a trap for you.'"

(New Century Version, Judges 2:1-3)

During the remarkable era of the 25th dynasty, a powerful unification occurred between Upper and Lower Egypt and Ethiopia. This vibrant period saw the revival of ancient Egyptian customs and spiritual beliefs. Under the rule of Taharka that the nation revitalized old religious manuscripts and wholeheartedly embraced the concept of a singular, true God. Taharka not only ended pagan worship across the country but also united citizens in their devotion to the Almighty Yahweh. Focusing on spiritual and educational growth, the Cushites created institutions for learning and rekindled their bond with the Israelites people.

CHAPTER FOUR

Ahab, Ahaz, and Hezekiah's Reigns in Israel and Judah

Ahab, a renowned king of Israel and the seventh in line was born to King Omri. His extraordinary leadership abilities were on par with the legendary King Solomon a hundred year prior. Like Solomon, Ahab's marriages introduced foreign beliefs to the Israelites, as he tried to satisfy his wife Jezebel, who was from Tyre, by permitting the worship of Baal alongside their original faith. Wanting to strengthen his ties with the Phoenicians and make his wife happy, Ahab constructed a wooden statue of the goddess Asherah. He took Ethbaal's cunning daughter as his bride - Ethbaal being the King of Tyre - which further solidified their alliance.

Ahab finished building the bustling capital city of Samaria, turning it into Israel's administrative heart. He breathed life back into the city of Hazor, making it a key military stronghold for defending the country's north. He fortified his kingdom for increased security by establishing more military outposts in Hazor and beyond. Ingeniously, a tunnel was carved near the mound's southern border to guarantee a reliable water source.

THE REIGN OF KING AHAB AND THE CONFLICT WITH ELIJAH

Under Ahab's rule, Israel thrived financially and became the top chariot builders in the area. Ahab strengthened Megiddo with a restored city wall and fortified gate while nurturing peace with Judah to the south. However, Ahab's downfall lay in his ties with idolatry. The Israelites lived among non-Jewish Canaanites, whom God had ordered them to drive out during the pre-exodus period. Yet, they defied God's command. Instead, they embraced Canaanite religious practices such as building shrines and performing Pagan rituals inherited from the Philistines. During Ahab's reign, Israel thrived, but the destructive influence of his wife Jezebel's idolatry cast a dark shadow over the nation. Ahab saw nothing wrong with participating in idol worship, and some Israelites followed suit, worshipping both the Canaanite gods and Yahweh. Ahab crafted wooden Asherah images and constructed an altar for Baal. He welcomed skilled foreign laborers to aid Israel's recovery while allowing them to worship Baal freely.

This embrace of Paganism led to corrupt practices. Jezebel cared little for the Lord, personifying the essence of her name and her god Baal: rebellion against God. She replaced Jewish sanctuaries with altars and shrines devoted to her Pagan deities and oppressed those who worshipped Yahweh. As Ahab took part in constructing Baal's altar, Elijah foresaw a devastating famine. He shared this prophecy with Ahab. "As the Lord God of Israel lives, before whom I stand; there shall not be dew nor rain these years, except at my word" (1 Kings 17:1).

The prophet Elijah openly criticized Ahab. When Ahab saw Elijah coming, Ahab said,

> *"17 ... Art thou he that troubleth Israel?*
> *18 And he answered, I have not troubled Israel;*
> *but thou, and thy father's house,*
> *in that ye have forsaken the commandments of the Lord,*
> *and thou hast followed Baalim."*
>
> *(King James Version, 1 Kings 18:17-18)*

Elijah boldly challenged the king to gather the 450 prophets of Baal and the 400 priests of Asherah, who dined at Jezebel's table, for a showdown. He declared, "How much longer will you waver between two beliefs? If the Lord is truly God, then follow Him."

> *21 And Elijah came to all the people, and said, "How long will you falter between two opinions? If the Lord is God, follow Him; but if Baal, follow him." But the people answered him not a word. 22 Then Elijah said to the people, "I alone am left a prophet of the Lord; but Baal's prophets are four hundred and fifty men. 23 Therefore let them give us two bulls; and let them choose one bull for themselves, cut it in pieces, and lay it on the wood, but put no fire under it; and I will prepare the other bull, and lay it on the wood, but put no fire under it. 24 Then you call on the name of your gods, and I will call on the name of the Lord; and the God who answers by fire, He is God." So, all the people answered and said, 5"It is well spoken."*
>
> *(The New King James Version, 1 Kings 18: 21-24)*

The Baal prophets readied the bull and called out to Baal all morning, pleading, "Baal, listen to us!" Elijah taunted them, saying, "Shout louder since he's a god! Maybe he's deep in thought, busy with something else, on a trip, or just taking a nap and needs waking up." Yet, there was still no response from Baal. Then Elijah said, "Come near to me." So, Elijah had the people put water over his sacrifice three separate times to prove there was no possibility of fraud. As Elijah called upon God, fiery flames descended from the sky, engulfing the burnt offering, wood, and stones. Astonishingly, even the water in the trench vaporized. Seeing this incredible sight, the Israelites dropped to their knees, begging for mercy. Without hesitation, Elijah addressed them. "Seize the prophets of Baal! Don't let one of them escape!" Thus, the Israelites escorted them from Mount Carmel to the Kishon River, where their execution occurred.

Elijah climbed to the peak of Mount Camel, seeking the Lord's guidance through prayer. He instructed his servant to descend the mountain toward the sea and search for rain seven times. Suddenly, a tiny cloud, no larger than a man's hand, emerged from the sea. The sky quickly darkened with clouds and gusty winds, followed by a downpour ending the drought (1 King 18:19-45). Upon learning about the terrible event, Jezebel was seething with anger and vowed to exact vengeance. Fearful, Elijah escaped to Mount Horeb and took shelter for the night in a cave. There, the Lord instructed Elijah to return to the city and face Ahab.

In her ruthless pursuit of power, Jezebel had Naboth, her neighbor, killed by stoning so that she could acquire his vineyard when he declined to sell it. Eventually, Elijah confronted Ahab at the vineyard. Overcome with shame, Ahab ripped his clothes apart and begged for forgiveness. It wasn't long before Ahab perished, fighting against Damascus, leaving his eldest son, Ahaziah, to inherit the throne.

Soon after becoming king, Ahaziah had a nasty fall from a balcony window in his Samaria palace. Injured and desperate, he sent messengers to consult the Philistine spiritual advisors and their god Baal-Zebub of Ekron about his recovery. On their way, they encountered Elijah, who gave them a prophecy to deliver to Ahaziah: "Is there no God in Israel that you seek help from Baal-Zebub? Because of this, you'll never leave your bed alive." Angered by Elijah's meddling, Ahaziah sent two squads of fifty men each to apprehend him, but both met a fiery end. Jehoram took the throne after Ahaziah and reigned in Israel for 12 years. Although he removed the Baal pillars, his mother Jezebel's Pagan influence persisted throughout Israel. Tragically, Jehoram met his end at the hands of his commander, Jehu, on Naboth the Jezreelite's land (2 Kings 9:21).

Elisha, Elijah's successor, anointed Jehu as king when Jehoram suffered injuries in battle at Ramoth Gilead. Jehu exterminated Ahab and Jezebel's entire household on a ruthless mission—relatives, servants, and friends alike. Jezebel was ousted out of a window by some eunuchs on Jehu's command. In a shocking turn of events, Jezebel's body faced the wrath of horses trampling her, followed by dogs devouring her remains. A grim discovery was made when only parts of her skull, hands, and feet were left to be buried. (2 Kings 9:32-36).

AHAZ'S REIGN AND THE FALL OF ISRAEL

Under King Ahaz's rule in Judah, he sought Assyria's protection against Damascus and Israel, led by Pekah. Despite being opposed to joining forces with Syria and Israel against Assyria, Ahaz paid taxes to the Assyrians for protection and adopted their Pagan practices. However, the prophet Isaiah warned Ahaz against aligning with Assyria and urged him to trust God.

In a shocking move, King Ahaz replaced the Lord's altar in Jerusalem's temple with that of a foreign deity. He crafted

Baal idols and offered child sacrifices in the Valley of Hinnom (2 Chron 28:1-4). Mesmerized by the gods of Damascus, Ahaz couldn't resist offering incense to various deities near a solitary evergreen tree. His devotion extended to sacrificing his sons to Rimmon—the Assyrian god—while dabbling in divination, witchcraft, and dark magic. As a result, Ahaz's wicked deeds deeply angered the Lord. Yet, he justified his actions by arguing that his worship of foreign gods aimed at winning the favor of the Syrian kings' deities. (2 Chron 28:23).

King Ahaz took treasures from the temple palaces of Judah to gain favor from his new ally and sought to join forces with Tiglath-Pilesar III, the Assyrian King. Despite the prophet Isaiah's warning that the alliance would fail and urging Ahaz to seek guidance from God, Ahaz declined, adamant not to test God. Consequently, he paid tributes using riches from Jerusalem's royal treasury and temple.

However, Israel and Syria united against Judah, invading the land effortlessly without Assyria's interference. They captured 200,000 Judeans as enslaved people and confiscated their possessions. As these soldiers approached Samaria, the prophet Oded met and spoke to them. Look, because the Lord God of your fathers was angry with Judah, He has delivered them into your hand; but you have killed them in a rage that reaches heaven. And now you propose to force the children of Judah and Jerusalem to be your male and female slaves, but are you not also guilty before the Lord your God? Therefore, hear me, and return the captives you have taken captive from your brethren, for the fierce wrath of the Lord is upon you.

Some Israelites bravely stood against the soldiers, offering food and shelter to the Judeans and granting them their freedom (2 Chron 28:9-10). Upon Ahaz's death, he was buried without a shred of honor in Jerusalem rather than in the tomb reserved for kings in Israel. Ahaz had plundered riches from the house of the Lord, the king's palace, and the leaders to appease the Assyrian king. But alas, his efforts were futile - Ahaz only grew more unfaithful to the Lord in his darkest moments.

> [17]*The LORD will bring on you and, on your people,*
> *and on the house of your father a time unlike*
> *any since Ephraim broke away from*
> *Judah—he will bring the king of Assyria."*
>
> *(New International Version,* Isaiah 7:17*)*

During the twelfth year of Ahaz's reign in Judah, King Hoshea seized the throne of the northern Kingdom of Israel. Thanks to Assyria's support, he rose to power after toppling King Pekah in Samaria. Pekah had previously defied Assyria's authority by withholding tribute. Both monarchs permitted their Assyrian counterparts to partake in idolatry. Capitalizing on Pekah's defiance and ensuing turmoil, Hoshea became a puppet king under Assyria.

In 732 B.C., Assyrian forces invaded Damascus, capturing the city and assassinating Syrian King Rezin. Countless Israelites were forcibly relocated out of their homeland by the conquering force. Following the death of Assyrian King Tiglath-Pilesar III, Hoshea ceased paying taxes to his domineering overlord and sought an alliance with Egypt. Upon learning of this betrayal, the new Assyrian King Shalmaneser retaliated against Israel, arresting Hoshea and imprisoning him.

Meanwhile, crowds of Israelites sought refuge behind the fortified walls of Samaria. Despite besieging the city relentlessly, the Assyrians failed to conquer it for three grueling years. In 721 BC., the Assyrian Army seized Samaria, Israel's last stronghold, taking its people captive. The city's buildings were destroyed, and soon, Assyrians settled the land. In the intervening time, the southern Kingdom of Judah cautiously expanded its power through political and economic alliances, offering protection to those who had escaped exile.

In 722 BC., the Assyrian King Shalmaneser passed away, and Sargon II took his place on the throne. During their conquest of Israel, the Assyrians imposed brutal punishments on high-ranking officials, such as disfiguring their bodies, gouging out their eyes, and even beheading or burning them alive. Numerous skilled workers and notable citizens were forcefully uprooted from their homeland and scattered across the empire. After these events, a rebellion broke out among the remaining Israelites in Israel. Sargon II swiftly returned in 720 BC., bringing with him the Assyrian Army. They proceeded to deport over 27,000 Israelites and replaced them with citizens from Assyria. During all this chaos, many surviving Israelites adopted the worship of Assyrian gods and merged with non-Jewish populations. Stories of some fleeing to Egypt and further into Africa slowly formed the well-known legend of the Ten Lost Tribes.

The last ruler of northern Israel was King Hoshea. Later, in 684 BC., Sennacherib seized power in Babylon during a revolt by flooding the city until it became a swampy wasteland. According to biblical accounts (2 Kings 17:20 and Isaiah 20:3-5), God ultimately rejected and punished Israel for their actions, leading to their dire fate at the hands of foreign captors.

HEZEKIAH'S RESISTANCE TO ASSYRIA AND MANASSEH'S WICKED REIGN

Upon inheriting the throne of Judah after Ahaz's passing, Hezekiah promptly set forth religious reformation and fostered a prosperous economy via trade and tax improvements. During his first year as ruler, he restored the house of the Lord, reopening the synagogue for worship. He invited the Israelite remnant to join Judah for Passover and eradicated idolatry by destroying wooden carvings and Moses' bronze serpent. As Egypt united with Ethiopia's twenty-fifth dynasty under King Shabaka, the Ethiopians conquered Egypt, executing Bocchoris and driving out Aryans. They annexed Philistia near Judah, while Merodach-Baladan, a Mesopotamian prince of the Bit-Yakin tribe, returned to Babylon, re-established himself on the throne, and regained Babylonian independence.

Capitalizing on a unique chance, Hezekiah defied Assyrian taxes and readied his people for war. Turning his attention on fortifying Judah, he confronted Assyria's ambitious conquests that had swallowed Syria and Israel while displacing many in Africa and Asia. Anticipating a clash with the mighty Assyrian army, Hezekiah cleverly built a tunnel to deprive them of water and struck an alliance with Ethiopia's king. Shabako ruled during this period, with Tirhakah leading Ethiopia's 25th dynasty. Preparing for a potential siege, Hezekiah ingeniously redirected water from Gihon spring into Siloam's walls. This tactic proved troublesome for the coalition when the Cushite warriors arrived without water supplies for their soldiers and horses.

In 701 BC., the Cushites attacked from the hills of Eltekeh along the Mediterranean Coast. Sennacherib collided with a large Ethiopian and Egyptian force armed with bows and horse-driven chariots at the city wall of Eltekeh. The Assyrians and the Cushites experienced heavy losses. The Ethiopians soon retreated, and Sennacherib destroyed the city. Instead of pursuing the Cushites, he focused on destroying nearby cities, digging ditches, and smashing tunnels and dams. He set the city on fire to stop the people from escaping and turned his attention to Babylon and Elam for their rebellion. Merodach-Baladan fled Kish to save his own life.

Sennacherib stormed into Eltekeh, Erech, Tyre, Sidon, and surrounding cities, ruthlessly executing rulers and nobles who took part in uprisings or denied paying tribute. He then confiscated their gold, silver, precious stones, and livestock. Having seized all valuable property, Sennacherib set the cities ablaze. His forces continued towards Ekron and Judah, overpowering the Ethiopian soldiers who had tried to assist. The ruthless Assyrians slaughtered city dwellers, staked out the cities' perimeter, and hung the corpses of defiant enemies on poles around the towns. Sennacherib's army then invaded the central highlands and targeted areas like the Sorek valley, Timnah, Mizpah, and Hittite lands along the Euphrates River and any native people unwilling to bow down to his authority.

All of the lands that quickly submitted to the Assyrians were forced to pay tribute, yet their lives were spared. Cities such as Ashdod, Ammon, Arvad, Edom, Gaza, and Pelusium presented extravagant gifts and noble daughters to the king, submitting by kissing his feet. The Assyrians believed their god, Indra the Asura, guided them in the battle against dark skin indigenous forces, compelling them to conquer their deity's foes. Sennacherib overcame being outnumbered and seized territories near Israel and Judah with the aid of mystical advisors and powerful military forces. Assyrians, like all Aryan conquerors, imposed their language and religion on those they defeated. They fearlessly fought on horseback and chariots, wielding long, two-handed swords and using bows from afar.

He verily, the god, the glorious Indra, hath raised him up for man...
brought low the dark head of the wicked Dasas...Indra the Vitra-slayer,
Fort destroyer, scattered the Dasa hosts who dwelt in darkness. To him
in might, the gods have ever yielded to Indra in the tumult of the battle.
When in his arms they laid the bolt, he slaughtered the Dasyus and cast
down their forts of iron (Griffith, 2008).

In the dramatic fourteenth year of King Hezekiah's rule, the relentless Assyrians attacked and took over 46 cities and 20 villages in Judah, including Lachish. Desperate to save his kingdom, Hezekiah sent messengers with a hefty offering of 300 talents of silver and 30 talents of gold to convince Sennacherib to halt his campaign (2 Kings 18:14). Meanwhile, the Ethiopian forces fought with Judah, but their struggles were far from over. They faced immense challenges in battle and had to retreat when the scorching heat became too much to bear. Hezekiah believed the Cushites had the skills to fight off Sennacherib's powerful army.

This partnership was crucial in resisting Aryan domination within their territories. However, ultimately, the Cushites lost their strength and capacity to challenge the mighty Assyrians. They had no choice but to surrender their remaining territories, marking the rule of white supremacy along the Nile. Boasting about his victory over a once-dominant force, Sennacherib proudly declared: "I have brought the black-headed people in submission at my feet."

Isaiah cautioned that even with the help of the Cushites, the deadly menace brought upon by the invaders wouldn't be stopped. The prowess of the Cushite Army had no bearing on the outcome of the clash between Judah and the ruthless, light-skinned invaders aiming to seize all land and belongings. Relying on Cushite support left Judah isolated and on a gradual decline. The Almighty God Yahweh had turned His gaze away. Sennacherib's pagan forces had humbled Judah and the Covenant nations: "Woe to those who seek help from Egypt, counting on horses, trusting in chariots because they are numerous, and in horsemen for their strength; yet overlooking the Holy One of Israel and not seeking the Lord!" (Isaiah 30:1)

Desperate to make amends, Hezekiah reached out to the Assyrian king after their forces withdrew. He offered precious gold stripped from the temple doors and cleared the palace's riches, but it failed to satisfy Sennacherib. Having conquered all of Judah except Jerusalem, Sennacherib stood triumphantly outside the city walls, praising his mighty Pagan god, Indra the Vitraslayer. Isaiah urged the people not to rely on their allies but instead to seek God's help for salvation. In response to Hezekiah's heartfelt prayer, the Lord intervened, annihilating 185,000 Assyrian soldiers.

> [20] *Then Isaiah son of Amoz sent a message to Hezekiah:*
> *"This is what the Lord, the God of Israel, says:*
> *I have heard your prayer concerning Sennacherib king of Assyria*
> *…and it came to pass…*
> [35] *That night the angel of the Lord went out and put to death a hundred and eighty-five thousand in the Assyrian camp. When the people got up the next morning—there were all the dead bodies!*
> *(New International Version, 2 Kings 19:20,35)*

Following the passing of Hezekiah, his son Manasseh ascended to the throne, becoming the fourteenth king of Judah. Known as one of Judah's most wicked and long-serving rulers, Manasseh's reign took after that of his grandfather, Ahaz. At 12 years old, he began his 55-year rule in Jerusalem, marked by heinous acts and abominations. Manasseh repeatedly crossed lines in defiance of the Lord, constructing altars for sun and star gods from Babylon and Nineveh within the sacred temple grounds. He emulated Ahab, King of Israel, by building altars for Baal and creating wooden idols.

Despite the Lord's declaration to establish His name in Jerusalem, Manasseh continued constructing unholy altars. He even went as far as rebuilding altars to worship pagan powers that his father had previously demolished. Manasseh sacrificed his sons to the god Molech in the Valley of Hinnom in a horrifying act. He dabbled in witchcraft, conversed with spirits, and committed acts deemed abominable by the Lord. Under Manasseh's cruel reign, the prophet Isaiah met his gruesome end — sawed in half. Manasseh paid tribute to Sennacherib and continued under Esarhaddon, who Sennacherib appointed governor of Babylon. Manasseh even provided troops against Ethiopia. The Ethiopians were Judah's most trusted and strongest allies but were Assyria's worst enemies. Much of Judah's gold came from the Cush area of Ophir.

During a temple worship service, Sennacherib met his end at the hands of his two sons, Adrammelech and Sharezer. They then fled to Ararat (2 Kings 19:37). With Sennacherib gone, his son Esarhaddon became king and united Assyria and Babylon. As the new ruler of Assyria, Esarhaddon focused on restoring Babylon. However, within the first year, Babylon revolted and sought Ethiopia as an ally. In 674 B.C., Esarhaddon led an attack against Ethiopian king Tirhakah but was defeated in Sais, Egypt. Esarhaddon shifted his focus to Judah, seizing King Manasseh and shackling him in bronze chains. He was then taken to Babylon, hooked, and imprisoned. In confinement, Manasseh showed humility to God. After being set free, he rid the Lord's house of all foreign deities and idols (2 Chronicles 33:11-15).

In 671 BC., Esarhaddon confronted Cushite King Tirhakah once more. He captured Memphis and numerous royal family members, including Tirhakah's wife and son. Necho I of Sais was appointed Egypt's puppet leader, pledging loyalty to the Assyrians. Consequently, Egypt had to pay tribute to Assyria. The allies depending on Egyptians for aid had to listen to Esarhaddon's boldness: "I am powerful, I am all-powerful, I am a hero, I am gigantic, I am colossal, I am honored, I am magnified, I am without an equal among all kings, the chosen one of Asshur, Nabu, and Marduk" (Walvoord & Zuck, 1983).

Esarhaddon permitted local leaders to retain their administrative roles in exchange for their assistance against the Cushites. Tirhakah retreated further south, gained backing from a few Egyptian rulers, and reclaimed Memphis after two years. Upon learning about the uprising, Esarhaddon rushed to Egypt but fell victim to an Ethiopian ambush. His son, Assurbanipal, took over and exacted revenge on the Egyptian conspirators.

Following Tirhakah's demise in 664 B.C., his nephew Tantamani, the final king of the twenty-fifth dynasty, led a march down the Nile into Egypt to eliminate Necho I. However, this triumph was short-lived, as a formidable Assyrian army overwhelmed Tantamani's forces. The Assyrians reconquered Lower Egypt, including Memphis, pushed towards Thebes, and seized immense treasures from Cush. The Assyrians installed Psammeticus I, the son of Necho I, as ruler of Lower Egypt forcing them to pay tribute. Still, Upper Egypt remained in Cushite control for another eight years. As punishment for defiance, many children and leading citizens of Egypt and Nubia were captured and executed.

In 656 B.C., Psamtik I brought Lower and Upper Egypt together, liberating the nation from Assyrian rule. Despite opposition from local leaders who preferred Cushite governance,

Psamtik formed strong economic and military bonds with Greece. He even established Greek settlements in Egypt, laying the foundation for a mighty kingdom. Egypt, boasting a powerful war fleet, dominated the Mediterranean and the Red Sea for over half a century.

CHAPTER FIVE

The Conquest of Babylon and the Tragic Fate of Kings

A s the Assyrian Empire's power diminished, Babylon's economy surged rapidly. Newcomers intermingled with the darker-skinned indigenous of Nineveh, while the Medes grew stronger from the north. The Prophet Nahum referred to Nineveh as "the city of blood," recognizing the Assyrians' brutal treatment of the indigenous people. During this time, numerous indigenous individuals were eager to resist Assyrian rule. To maintain control, the population faced extreme cruelty, such as impalement, decapitation, and even child burnings. These acts only fueled their determination to join forces with Babylon.

THE FALL OF NINEVEH AND THE BABYLONIAN REVOLT

In 652 BC., a dramatic revolt unfolded as Shamash-shum-ukin, the ruler of Babylon, rebelled against his brother,

Assurbanipal. Despite their efforts, Babylon succumbed to starvation and conceded defeat. In response, Assurbanipal appointed two family members as co-governors of Babylon. Upon Assurbanipal's death in 627 BC., the tides shifted when Nabopolassar, an ex-Assyrian general, seized power in Babylon and pushed out the relatives. Crowned king in 626 BC., he joined forces with Cyaxares, the King of Medes, to wage war against Assyria. King Josiah of Judah sided with Assyria, hoping this alliance would benefit his kingdom. Josiah tried to halt Egypt's advance through Mount Carmel by aiding the Assyrians against Babylon in a bold move. He clashed with Necho II in a fierce battle at Megiddo, suffering severe injuries. Josiah retreated to Jerusalem but ultimately succumbed to his wounds. The Medes and Babylonians stormed into Nineveh, destroying the city and forcing many residents into exile. Jehoahaz took over as king after Josiah but was swiftly arrested by Necho II in Riblah three months into his reign. Necho II then conquered Judah and appointed Jehoiakim, Jehoahaz's brother, the new king.

> [20] *After all this, when Josiah had prepared the temple,*
> *Necho king of Egypt came up to fight against*
> *Carchemish by the Euphrates; and Josiah went out against him.*
> [21] *But he sent messengers to him, saying, "What have I to do with you,*
> *king of Judah? I have not come against you this day, but against the*
> *house with which I have war; for God commanded me to make haste.*
> *Refrain from meddling with God, who is with me, lest He destroy you."*
> [23] *And the archers shot King Josiah; and the king said to his servants,*
> *"Take me away, for I am severely wounded."*
>
> *(New King James Version, 2 Chronicles 35:20-21,23)*

JUDAH'S FUTURE PROPHECIES AND WARNINGS

In the 18th year of King Josiah's rule, the High Priest Hilkiah uncovered the long-lost "Book of the Law," confirming the Jews' storied past. This revelation prompted a religious revolution, and Josiah was shocked to see how far his people had strayed from God's law. The king promptly dismantled all Baal altars and Pagan idols, purifying Judah and Israel from idol-worship and immoral customs like ritual prostitution. He also established a unified form of worship. Josiah was merely eight when he became king, reigning over Judah for 31 years before King Jehoiakim took control. This new ruler fell short, disregarding justice and embracing idolatry during his reign from 609 to 598 BC. He angered God in doing so and faced heavy taxation from Egypt. In response to this dire situation, the Lord instructed the prophet Jeremiah to send a powerful message to the people of Judah, saying:

> [2] "Thus says the Lord: 'Stand in the court of the Lord's house,
> and speak to all the cities of Judah, which come
> to worship in the Lord's house, all the words
> that I command you to speak to them. Do not diminish a word.
> [3] Perhaps everyone will listen and turn from his evil way,
> that I may relent concerning the calamity which
> I purpose to bring on them because of the evil of their doings.'
> [6] then I will make this house like Shiloh,
> and will make this city a curse to all the nations of the earth." ' "
>
> *(New King James Version, Jeremiah 26:2-3,6)*

After Jeremiah finished his conversation with the priest, the false prophets demanded his capture. He spoke up, explaining that God tasked him to warn Judah and nearby Covenant nations. He urged them to change their ways and follow God's commandments. Jeremiah offered himself as punishment, but some elders defended him. God instructed Jeremiah to wear a wooden yoke publicly, signifying submission to Babylon. He sent bonds and yokes to six neighboring nations allied with Babylon, who were once deemed Israel's siblings by the prophets. Prophet Amos criticized them for breaking the Covenant of Brotherhood. The Ammonites and Moabites descended from Lot, while the Edomites came from Esau's interracial marriages. They all grew hostile towards the Jews and often sided against them. Jeremiah's presence in the temple encouraged rival prophet Hananiah to deliver a counter-prophecy. He seized the wooden yoke from Jeremiah and broke it in defiance. Subsequently, Jeremiah returned wearing an iron yoke around his neck.

[13] "Go and tell Hananiah, saying, 'Thus says the Lord:

"You have broken the yokes of wood,

but you have made in their place yokes of iron."

[14] For thus says the Lord of hosts, the God of Israel:

"I have put a yoke of iron on the neck of all these nations, that they may serve Nebuchadnezzar king of Babylon; and they shall serve him.

I have given him the beasts of the field also." ' "

[15] Then the prophet Jeremiah said to Hananiah the prophet,

"Hear now, Hananiah, the Lord has not sent you,

but you make this people trust in a lie.

[16] Therefore thus says the Lord: 'Behold, I will cast you from the face of the earth.

This year you shall die, because you have taught rebellion against the Lord.' "

[17] So Hananiah the prophet died the same year in the seventh month.

(New King James Version, Jeremiah 28: 13-16)

Hananiah spoke boldly with an opposing prophecy: "Thus says the Lord: 'Even so I will break the yoke of Nebuchadnezzar king of Babylon from the neck of all the nations within the space of two full years.' In 605 BC., a legendary battle occurred at Carchemish, where the Assyrians defeated the Egyptians. Following their victory, Babylon seized crucial Egyptian territories like Ashkelon. Jehoiakim decided to bow to Babylon's power and pay tribute to King Nebuchadnezzar to safeguard Judah from attack. As a result, important members of Judah's royal family - such as Daniel and his close friends Hananiah, Mishael, and Azariah - were captured and taken to Babylon. Their names were changed to Shadrach, Meshach, and Abed-Nego to erase their Hebrew identity and absorb them into Chaldean society.

Meanwhile, Ethiopia was absent from this historic battle. Earlier rulers, Necho I and Psammeticus I had severed Egypt's connection with Ethiopia due to their fear of the Assyrians. Many Egyptians, including soldiers, chose to side with Ethiopia instead, harboring deep resentment towards the cruel Assyrians.

The Battle of Carchemish breathed new life into Judah as Assyrian forces and a fraction of the Philistines joined Egyptian forces to confront Babylon bravely. In doing so, they managed to prevent Egypt's downfall, allowing them to continue their fight. Three years later, Jehoiakim broke away from Nebuchadnezzar and allied Judah with Egypt again. Subsequently, Babylon's allies – the Chaldeans, Syrians, and Ammonites – launched an attack on Judea and put it under siege without any intervention from Egypt. King Jehoiakim of Judah passed away just before the final confrontation took place. With him, the prophet Ezekiel was taken captive.

Babylon's partners encircled Judah, allowing Nebuchadnezzar and his forces to deal a crushing blow. Anticipating this strike, newly crowned King Jeconiah, the royal family, and Judah's officers conceded defeat to the Babylonian king. Consequently, Nebuchadnezzar pillaged sacred treasures and golden artifacts from their temple. The Babylonian ruler then seized all artisans and skilled laborers, leaving only the most impoverished among Judah's citizens. King Jeconiah's reign would be tragically short-lived – after just three months as leader, he was deported to Babylon. Nebuchadnezzar took Jeconiah captive and appointed his uncle, Mattaniah, king of Judah. Nebuchadnezzar changed his name to Zedekiah. After Jeconiah's exile, God showed Jeremiah two baskets of figs.

3 Then the Lord said to me, "What do you see, Jeremiah?" And I said, "Figs, the good figs, very good; and the bad, very bad, which cannot be eaten, they are so bad."

4 Again the word of the Lord came to me, saying,

5 "Thus says the Lord, the God of Israel: 'Like these good figs, so will I acknowledge those who are carried away captive from Judah, whom I have sent out of this place for their own good, into the land of the Chaldeans.

6 For I will set My eyes on them for good, and I will bring them back to this land; I will build them and not pull them down, and I will plant them and not pluck them up.

7 Then I will give them a heart to know Me, that I am the Lord; and they shall be My people, and I will be their God, for they shall return to Me with their whole heart.

8 'And as the bad figs which cannot be eaten, they are so bad'--surely thus says the Lord--'so will I give up Zedekiah the king of Judah, his princes, the residue of Jerusalem who remain in this land, and those who dwell in the land of Egypt.

⁹ I will deliver them to trouble into all the kingdoms of the earth, for their harm, to be a reproach and a byword, a taunt and a curse, in all places where I shall drive them.

(New King James Version, Jeremiah 24:2-9)

As Zedekiah began his reign, he faced enormous pressure to rebel against Nebuchadnezzar. Despite this, he pledged loyalty to Babylon for nine years. The persistent urging of his people and religious leaders and support from a new Egyptian pharaoh made it tough for him. Seeking guidance, Zedekiah turned to Jeremiah, who advised him to submit to Babylonian rule.

⁷ "Thus says the Lord, the God of Israel,
'Thus you shall say to the king of Judah,
who sent you to Me to inquire of Me:
"Behold, Pharaoh's army which has come up
to help you will return to Egypt, to their own land.
⁸ And the Chaldeans shall come back and fight against this city,
and take it and burn it with fire." '

(New King James Version, Jeremiah 37:7-8)

King Nebuchadnezzar and his mighty army surrounded Judah with a strong siege wall. As time went on, food grew scarce, and the people suffered terribly. However, when word spread, that Egyptian soldiers were coming to aid Judah, the Babylonians retreated in fear of Pharaoh's military power. After the relentless siege, many individuals, including Jeremiah, left Jerusalem. As Jeremiah approached the Gates of Benjamin, he was unexpectedly arrested and accused of being a traitor. He was thrown into a dark dungeon until the king heard about his arrest. Wanting to show mercy, the king moved him to the Court of Prison instead. Zedekiah asked Jeremiah for advice, and he again gave them prophecy, saying, Thus, says the Lord: "He who remains in this city shall die by the sword, famine, and pestilence; but he who goes over to the Chaldeans shall live; his life shall be as a prize to him, and he shall live." Thus, says the Lord: "This city shall surely be given into the hand of the king of Babylon's army, which shall take it."

Jeremiah was moved to a grimy dungeon with no water, only sludge. An Ethiopian guard, a eunuch, heard about Jeremiah's plight and begged the king for his release. Thus, the king sent 30 men alongside Ebed-Melech, the Ethiopian, to rescue Jeremiah from the dungeon. Zedekiah secretly approached Jeremiah and promised safety in exchange for a final prophecy about Judah.

> [17] *Then Jeremiah said to Zedekiah,*
> *"Thus says the Lord, the God of hosts, the God of Israel:*
> *'If you surely surrender to the king of Babylon's princes,*
> *Then your soul shall live; this city shall not be burned with fire,*
> *and you and your house shall live.*
> [18] *But if you do not surrender to the king of Babylon's princes,*
> *then this city shall be given into the hand of the Chaldeans;*
> *they shall burn it with fire, and you shall not escape from their hand.'"*
> *(New King James Version, Jeremiah 38: 17-18)*

The Jewish people who fled to Babylon didn't like Zedekiah because they still saw Jeconiah as their true king. Zedekiah once promised to free all Hebrew enslaved people, but he went back on his word. When the Babylonians returned to Jerusalem, the king and his advisors waited until dark before trying to get away. They managed to sneak through a hole in the city wall and aimed for the king's garden. However, the Babylonian army chased after King Zedekiah and caught him in the open fields of Jericho. They took him to Nebuchadnezzar, where he was forced to watch his sons die. After that, they blinded him, shackled him in bronze, and dragged him off to Babylon.

The Babylonians captured and executed Judah's political, religious, and military leaders. They raided the palaces and took valuable items like bronze, gold, and pots. The Babylonians then set fire to the temple, the king's palace, and all the prominent homes in Jerusalem. Nebuzaradan, a high-ranking guard, led the hostages out of the city. However, some poor people were left behind to tend to the land as vineyard workers and farmers.

> *⁹ Ethiopia and Egypt were her strength,*
> *And it was boundless; Put and Lubim were your helpers.*
> *¹⁰ Yet she was carried away, She went into captivity;*
> *Her young children also were dashed to pieces*
> *At the head of every street; They cast lots for her honorable men,*
> *And all her great men were bound in chains.*
>
> *(New King James Version, Nahum 3:9-10)*

In place of Jerusalem, the Babylonians created a local government in Mizpah and made Gedaliah the governor of Judah. Jeremiah, found in prison and chained, was taken to Babylon with other captives. Nebuchadnezzar ordered Nebuzarian to spare Jeremiah and treated him kindly. After being set free, Jeremiah was chosen to go anywhere, including Babylon, where he would be well-treated due to his prophecy against Judah that made Nebuchadnezzar see him as an ally. Many Jews escaped to nearby Ammon, Moab, Edom, Egypt, or the wilderness to avoid Babylon's fury. However, when they heard about Gedaliah being governor, several Jews decided to return to Judah. Tragically, Ishmael and ten others plotted against Gedaliah and assassinated him and other Jewish people and political leaders. Ishmael fled to Ammon, while some Jews escaped Egypt fearing the Babylonians' reactions.

Just like the Babylonians, the Assyrian Aryans also adopted Babylon as their homeland instead of the European mountains. Babylon was likely the first Aryan region to welcome people with darker skin into various aspects of society, such as politics, religion, military, and economy. These individuals had the opportunity to farm, serve in the army, and work as merchants or traders. They could even purchase their freedom from slavery. However, Nebuchadnezzar still enslaved Hebrews to construct lavish palaces and hanging gardens. The Book of Revelation depicts Babylon as a seductive temptress, luring people away from God with its luxurious and prestigious lifestyle. This majestic kingdom is brimming with pride and beauty, earning it the title of the first "beast" in the Book of Daniel. As a powerful nation, Babylon holds sway over political governments through its military might, cunning manipulation, and oppressive systems.

In its quest for supremacy, Babylon cleverly used tactics like divide and conquer. It lured the Hebrews with enticing opportunities, only to betray and enslave its darker-skinned allies, much like the oppression of Judah. "Babylon" means "Gateway to the gods," believed to be where fallen angels first divulged secret knowledge to humanity. The Aryans later tapped into this sinister power to take revenge on the Covenant nations.

> *It is the devils who are unbelievers they teach men witchcraft and that which was revealed to the angels Harut and Marut in Babylon.*
>
> (Koran: The Cow 2:102)

And in the Bible;

⁹ So the great dragon was cast out, that serpent of old,
called the Devil and Satan, who deceives the whole world; he was cast to
the earth, and his angels were cast out with him.

(New King James Version, Revelation 12:9*)*

The Hebrew people settled in colonies or small municipalities along the Chebar River, a large waterway flowing along the southeast of Babylon. Once Jeconiah was freed, Evil-Merodach took the throne and became close friends with Jeconiah. Together, they built a thriving community in Nehardea, complete with a fancy residence and a synagogue. Jews in the area flourished both socially and financially. Though many captives could wander freely around Babylon, the Babylonians wanted to remind the Hebrews that their Pagan gods still ruled. So, they built an enormous 44,000-pound golden statue of Marduk sitting on a royal throne, making it crystal clear who held power in Babylon. Marduk was the head honcho amongst the gods worshipped there, always at the center of religious ceremonies.

During the vibrant Akitu festival, Nebo's (Nabu) statue made a grand journey from Borsippa to Babylon's Esagila Temple, signifying the union of two mighty gods. As the god of wisdom and writing, and Marduk's son, Nabo played a key role in rallying the gods to join forces with Marduk, ensuring Babylon's divine protection from evil for the upcoming year. Eagerly anticipating this grand event, the king was accompanied by priests to the temple, where they presented sacred offerings to the heavenly beings. With an intense focus on ancient rituals, the temple was cleansed and consecrated for this sacred occasion.

The Akitu festival marked the arrival of spring and its rejuvenating power and signaled the start of the Babylonian new year. These mystical rites and celebratory gatherings invoked a harmonious bond between cosmic forces and humanity's place in the universe. One fascinating ancient celebration was the Bacchus festival, held to honor the birth of the queen of heaven's son. Bacchus, the god of wine and fertility, was linked to love, sacred relationships, and nature's fertility cycles.

In Babylonian lore, Ishtar was the heavenly queen, and her son Tammuz symbolized the changing seasons through his annual death and miraculous rebirth. The Bacchus, also known as the intoxicated festival, featured the positive effects of wine, dancing, and holy personal interactions for purifying sins. A myth stated that engaging in these activities with temple worshippers would gain approval from the gods. It was a common practice for young women to dedicate their first intimate experience to the great mother goddess during fertility rites. Starting around December 21st, this five-day event allowed enslaved people temporary freedom and complete autonomy.

In times of peace, they donned vibrant purple robes, while leopard skins were their attire for war. They adorned an evergreen tree with luxurious gold and silver embellishments and ribbons as part of their customs. The mystical mistletoe branch was merged with the earthly tree to symbolize heavenly harmony. These magical festivities were known to bestow divine blessings upon humanity.

In Hindu and Babylonian myths, the evergreen tree symbolized revival and the awareness of life. They prepared special cakes, bouns, or buns, which they offered to their ancestors' spirits during gift exchanges to honor celestial beings. In the Book of Daniel, Belshazzar likely attended a lively Bacchus festival when the writing on the wall appeared. Romans used to rejoice during their December festival, Saturnalia, and celebrated Bacchus in March - each lasting five days. The Roman calendar had only ten months, with March marking the

New Year's beginning. However, Julius Caesar introduced the Julian calendar in 46 B.C., adding January and February.

In 186 BC., Rome's Senate banned the wild and senseless festivals due to their immoral nature, causing many people to carry on with the celebrations secretly. Later on, these festivals were brought back and permitted under the watchful eye of the Roman government. Interestingly, the Hebrews also partook in this Pagan practice that upset God. Nowadays, Christmas shares several similarities with the Bacchus festival, such as honoring the evergreen tree, with women being major contributors to this tradition.

> [16] *"Therefore do not pray for this people, nor lift up a cry or prayer for them,*
> *nor make intercession to Me; for I will not hear you.*
> [17] *Do you not see what they do in the cities of Judah and in the streets of Jerusalem?*
> [18] *The children gather wood, the fathers kindle the fire, and the women knead dough, to make cakes for the queen of heaven; and they pour out drink offerings to other gods, that they may provoke Me to anger.*
> *(New King James Version, Jeremiah 7:16-18).*

> [1] *Belshazzar the king made a great feast for a thousand of his lords, and drank wine in the presence of the thousand.*
> [4] *They drank wine, and praised the gods of gold and silver, bronze and iron, wood and stone.*
> [5] *In the same hour the fingers of a man's hand appeared and wrote opposite the lampstand on the plaster of the wall of the king's palace; and the king saw the part of the hand that wrote.*
> *(New King James Version, Daniel 5:1,4-5)*

Babylon, a magnificent city, featured eight grand bronze gates and towering walls that reached 320 feet in height and 80 feet in thickness. Moreover, a waterway fully surrounded the city. The Ishtar Gate, adorned with dazzling enamel bricks, was the majestic northern entrance, depicting images of a lion, dragon, and bull. Processional Street Road stretched from the eastern side of the Southern Palace towards the Ishtar Gate. It held the Nabo Temple at its southern end to pay tribute to the god of wisdom. Aibur-shabu, another road, passed through the impressive Ishtar Gate between two tall walls. Both streets were paved with gorgeous breccia limestone from the mountains by Nebuchadnezzar.

Small red marble stones lined the sidewalks, while massive breccia rocks embellished the center of the roads. Representing Mother Earth was Ishtar, and her son Tammuz symbolized fertility. A Tammuz statue stood at the temple's Northern gate where Ezekiel once envisioned a Judean woman mourning for the pagan deity. The ziggurats, or temples, were awe-inspiring structures resembling pyramids that towered nearly 300 feet high. The king's main palace and official residence was the Esagila Temple, the Southern Palace. A mighty fortress was strategically located between the Ishtar Gate and the Euphrates River, with a seven-story watchtower guarding the city from above.

Babylon's renowned hanging gardens were likely situated on the top and along the stairway of the Southern Palace. These captivating gardens featured a variety of trees, flowers, and vines supported by immense marble and limestone pillars, complete with an artificial waterfall mimicking Medo-Persia's mountainous terrain. King Nebuchadnezzar is believed to have constructed these enchanting gardens to please one of his wives, who deeply cherished her homeland.

Nebuchadnezzar gathered Babylon's most brilliant artists and innovators for his grand endeavors. He proudly displayed his inscriptions on the city's walkways, showcasing his achievements. However, it was African and enslaved Israelites who constructed these magnificent projects. They could earn their freedom in exchange for contributing their skills to make Babylon the world's most breathtaking city. Babylon flourished with extraordinary pride and allure, excelling in military, political, and economic realms. Many Hebrews grew wealthy by capitalizing on the fertile land between the kingdom's three major cities – Babylon, Nippur, and Kish. It appeared that Nebuchadnezzar aimed to seduce them into adopting a Babylonian identity over their Hebrew roots. Many Hebrews were unaware of their heritage, which is why Psalm 137 poetically reminded them of their true origins.

¹By the rivers of Babylon,
There we sat down, yea, we wept
When we remembered Zion.
²We hung our harps
Upon the willows in the midst of it.
³For those who carried us
Away captive asked of us a song,
And those who plundered us requested mirth,
Saying, "Sing us one of the songs of Zion!"
⁴How shall we sing the Lord's song in a foreign land?
If I do not remember you,
⁶Let my tongue cling to the roof of my mouth
If I do not exalt Jerusalem

(New King James Version, Psalms 137: 1-4,6)

Nebuchadnezzar experienced a bizarre dream with significant implications during his second year as king. Eager to understand its meaning, he called upon his magicians, astrologers, and wise men who claimed to possess divine abilities. However, the king decided to test their true powers. He announced, "I've had a dream that leaves my spirit restless, longing for an interpretation."

> [5] *The king answered and said to the Chaldeans,*
> *"My decision is firm: if you do not make known the dream to me,*
> *and its interpretation, you shall be cut in pieces,*
> *and your houses shall be made an ash heap.*
> [6] *However, if you tell the dream and its interpretation,*
> *you shall receive from me gifts, rewards, and great honor.*
> *Therefore tell me the dream and its interpretation."*
>
> (*New King James Version,* Daniel 2: 5-6)

One of the Chaldeans spoke to the king in Aramaic: "O king live forever! Tell your servants the dream, and we will give the interpretation."

The king's request seemed impossible to the astrologers, believing only the gods could provide an answer. The king's anger led him to order the execution of the wise men. Arioch, the head of the guards, informed Daniel about this decree. Daniel persuaded Arioch to let him speak with the king and asked for time to interpret the king's dream. Daniel and his friends prayed fervently for God's mercy, asking Him to unveil the king's secret to save them from their fate. Miraculously, that very night, God revealed both the vision and its interpretation to Daniel through a dream. Grateful for God's intervention, Daniel offered heartfelt thanks to the Heavenly Lord.

> [20] *Daniel answered and said:*
> *"Blessed be the name of God forever and ever,*
> *For wisdom and might are His.*
> *wisdom and might are His.*

²¹ And He changes the times and the seasons;

He removes kings and raises up kings;

He gives wisdom to the wise And knowledge to those who have understanding.

²² He reveals deep and secret things;

He knows what is in the darkness, And light dwells with Him.

²³ "I thank You and praise You, O God of my fathers; You have given me wisdom and might, And have now made known to me what we asked of You, For You have made known to us the king's demand."

(New King James Version, Daniel 2:20-23)

After finishing his prayer, Daniel approached Arioch and urged him not to harm the wise men, promising to interpret the king's dream. He started by crediting God, telling the king that even the most skilled wise men, astrologers, magicians, or soothsayers couldn't uncover the dream's mystery. However, a God in heaven divulged secrets, and this divine being shared the dream with Daniel. With that knowledge, Daniel began recounting the king's dream in detail.

²⁹ As for you, O king, thoughts came to your mind while on your bed, about what would come to pass after this;

and He who reveals secrets has made known to you what will be.

³⁰ But as for me, this secret has not been revealed to me because I have more wisdom than anyone living, but for our sakes who make known the interpretation to the king, and that you may know the thoughts of your heart.

³¹ "You, O king, were watching; and behold, a great image! This great image, whose splendor was excellent, stood before you; and its form was awesome.

³² This image's head was of fine gold, its chest and arms of silver, its belly and thighs of bronze,

³³ its legs of iron, its feet partly of iron and partly of clay.

34 You watched while a stone was cut out without hands, which struck the image on its feet of iron and clay, and broke them in pieces.

35 Then the iron, the clay, the bronze, the silver, and the gold were crushed together, and became like chaff from the summer threshing floors; the wind carried them away so that no trace of them was found. And the stone that struck the image became a great mountain and filled the whole earth.

36 "This is the dream..."

(New King James Version, Daniel 2:29-36)

Daniel explained to the king that Babylon was the start of four great empires, symbolized by the golden head granted to him by God. After Babylon's fall, a second kingdom, weaker than Babylon and represented by the silver chest and arms, would follow. Next, a third kingdom would rule the world, symbolizing the bronze body born from the sea people.

Lastly, a fourth kingdom characterized by iron legs and feet would conquer others. Although this kingdom would shatter into fragments, it would still consume all other kingdoms on Earth. The realm would be divided, but the power of iron would prevail in each conquered piece of the fallen domains. A peculiar creature with four heads was granted the ability to govern the earth. The fourth beast stood out from the rest, possessing incredible strength. It had massive teeth for tearing and crushing flesh, and as it did so, remnants would scatter on the ground. This odd creature also had ten horns, among which a smaller one emerged, featuring human-like eyes and a mouth uttering grand pronouncements. This little horn grew swiftly, casting a shadow over the lesser ones.

The fourth kingdom, Rome, is symbolized by its legs, feet, and fragile ten toes. A portion of this fallen empire would persistently reign supreme while maintaining Rome's influence until the arrival of the Messiah. These kingdoms were stronger than gold, silver, or bronze due to their iron-like nature but also partly frail because of their intolerance. The Gentile kingdoms comprised people from the Balkans who settled in Babylon, Medo-Persia, Greece, and Rome (Daniel 2:37-45).

While Greeks excelled intellectually, philosophically, and culturally, Roman societies contrasted with them. Romans inherited more enslaved people than Greeks and employed them in agriculture; they also mastered animal domestication. As a result of these skills, Rome rose to power and managed to rule over Greek city-states.

As Greece valiantly battled the Persians, drawing their forces away from the mainland, Rome prepared its citizen soldiers on daring missions to defend Greece. Rapidly expanding, Rome devised a strategy to categorize its people into five groups based on their riches. During the Golden Age of Greece, people unlocked the universe's secrets through philosophy and science while embracing innovative ideas. Meanwhile, ancient Rome grew wealthy, with an abundance of luxurious buildings, establishments, and public amenities reflecting their superior way of life. The Roman Empire eventually splintered into ten separate countries, including Britain.

These new nations, bound together by their unyielding nature, embarked on ruthless conquests to expand their territories. As a result, they turned into merciless forces against any nation that opposed their military and political aspirations. Daniel encountered a fierce beast with ten horns, representing ten kingdoms. These kingdoms battled one another until a small horn emerged as a powerful mediator. This little horn eliminated its competition—three weaker horns—and amassed enough wealth and authority to intervene among Rome's divided territories.

The small horn possessed human-like eyes and a mouth that spoke boastfully, made from potter's clay. As time passed since Daniel's vision, the papacy of Rome evolved into a church and state union with significant control over various government affairs and religious institutions in Western Europe. The reach of Rome's papacy extended to the Middle East, Africa, and even the United States. The United States emerged from the British Empire with immense military, political, and economic might. Similar to Rome, the US adopted the eagle as its official symbol.

CHAPTER SIX

Dreams, Madness, and Redemption in the Life of King Nebuchadnezzar

A stone, magically cut from a mountain, shattered the images, overtook all kingdoms, and stood eternal. Daniel's profound spiritual wisdom astonished King Nebuchadnezzar as he unveiled the king's dream and meaning. Humbly bowing to Daniel, the king promoted him to ruler and chief administrator throughout Babylon. Nebuchadnezzar shared another dream with Daniel - a mighty tree reaching heaven, visible to all on Earth. Its leaves were beautiful, its fruits plentiful. The tree sheltered wild animals below and offered a haven for birds among its branches.

[23] *And inasmuch as the king saw a watcher, a holy one, coming down from heaven and saying, 'Chop down the tree and destroy it, but leave its stump and roots in the earth, bound with a band of iron and bronze in the tender grass of the field; let it be wet with the dew of heaven, and let him graze with the beasts of the field, till seven times pass over him';*

(*New King James Version*, Daniel 4:23)

Nebuchadnezzar's Humility and Restoration

The dream of the king left Daniel shocked and puzzled for a moment. He reassured Nebuchadnezzar not to worry about the dream or its meaning. Daniel suggested that perhaps the dream related to the king's enemies and those who despised him, but deep down, he knew it was meant for the king himself. Daniel was honest and straightforward about this. Daniel explained to Nebuchadnezzar that God planned to cast him out from humanity and that he would live among wild animals, eating grass like an ox. The king was to experience this for a specific period until he understood that God ruled over all kingdoms and granted them to those He chose. Once the king recognized divine rule, his kingdom would be restored.

Daniel advised Nebuchadnezzar to renounce his sins by embracing righteousness and forsaking his wrongdoings by showing kindness to the less fortunate to increase his chances of prolonging his prosperity. This way, perhaps God would extend the king's wealth and success (Daniel 4:19-27). The following year, King Nebuchadnezzar lost recall of the dream and its interpretation given to him by Daniel. One day, he strolled around his magnificent palace, marveling at the city of Babylon below. Standing at the Southern Palace near the towering 300-foot Esagila Temple, he could see a vast expanse of his city.

The mesmerizing Hanging Gardens bloomed on the palace rooftop while the mighty Euphrates River wound through Babylon, serving as a protector and provider. Overwhelmed with pride, Nebuchadnezzar exclaimed, "Isn't this glorious Babylon I've built as my royal home with my incredible strength, all to showcase my royal splendor?"

> *[31] While the word was still in the king's mouth, a voice fell from heaven: "King Nebuchadnezzar, to you it is spoken: the kingdom has departed from you!*
> *[32] And they shall drive you from men, and your dwelling shall be with the beasts of the field. They shall make you eat grass like oxen; and seven times shall pass over you, until you know that the Most High rules in the kingdom of men,*
> *and gives it to whomever He chooses."*
>
> *(New King James Version, Daniel 4: 31-32)*

King Nebuchadnezzar lost his mind in that fateful hour and was cast out of the palace. He lived like a wild animal, eating grass soaked by dew, with hair like an eagle's feathers and nails that resembled bird claws. This madness lasted seven long years before he finally regained his sanity. Once he returned to his senses, he praised the God of Heaven and realized that God's kingdom lasts forever. The king acknowledged that his downfall was due to his pride and learned that even the most powerful could be humbled. With this lesson, he regained his honored position, happily welcomed back by those under his rule.

A second dream made Nebuchadnezzar understand that his god, Marduk, paled in comparison to the Almighty. After a 43-year reign, his son, Abilmathadachos, succeeded him on the throne. Before Babylon's fall, the Book of Daniel introduced us to the Crown Prince, Nebuchadnezzar's grandson, Belshazzar. His father, Nabonidus, was the last king of Babylon. With his marriage to Nebuchadnezzar's daughter, Nitocris, Nabonidus secured his kingship after Laboroarchod's death, a nine-month reign. Historian Herodotus said Nitocris' mother might have been from Egyptian royalty during a failed invasion in 569 BC.

Nitocris was considered an illegitimate child since her mom was labeled a widow. Chances are that her mom may have been one of Nebuchadnezzar's concubines. Victory often led to rulers claiming defeated enemies' wives and daughters as concubines or harlots – a form of humiliation.

Nabonidus established the moon god Sin as Babylon's primary deity, which led to ongoing clashes with religious authorities who favored Marduk. He relocated his royal residence to Tema in northern Arabia to escape the conflict. He constructed temples in his hometown, Haran - where Abraham's father, Terah, halted his journey to Canaan. This decision to live in Haran displeased God, as Joshua relayed: "The Lord God of Israel says, 'Your ancestors, including Terah – Abraham and Nahor's father – lived across the Euphrates River in ancient times and worshipped other gods.'"

> [3] *Then I took your father Abraham from the other side of the River,*
> led him throughout all the land of Canaan,
> and multiplied his descendants and gave him Isaac.
>
> *(New King James Version,* Joshua 24:2-3*)*

Nabonidus skipped the Akitu, the famous Babylonian New Year Festival, angering priests, officials, and locals. Leaving his son Belshazzar in charge for a decade, they both banked on their past successes to protect their kingdom. Upon Nabonidus's return three years before Cyrus's attack, he found Babylon in disarray. Once allies with Persia and the Medes against the Assyrians, Babylon faced an unexpected betrayal. Darius (Gobryas), a Babylonian governor of Elam on Persia's border, joined forces with Cyrus. After defeating the Medes, Persia set its sights on conquering Babylonian cities.

Nabonidus stationed his troops and officials in Akkad,

while Belshazzar stood guard in Babylon. As Cyrus targeted the forces at Opis along the Tigris River, Akkad's people rebelled. The Persians, led by Darius, crushed the uprising in Akkad and took control of Sippar. Upon seeing Darius, his chosen governor, turn against him, Nabonidus fled. Meanwhile, Belshazzar was preoccupied with a grand feast alongside his officers, wives, and concubines at the royal palace. He mocked God by drinking from the holy vessels plundered from Jerusalem's temples during Nebuchadnezzar's invasion. As they drank and indulged, they celebrated their past triumphs and praised their deities.

One day, Belshazzar saw mysterious writing on the palace wall and became terrified. He yelled for Babylon's wisest men to decipher it, but none could make sense of the words. Amidst the chaos in the banquet hall, the queen remembered a Judean dream interpreter whom Belshazzar's grandfather had favored. Belshazzar called for Daniel and offered him royal rewards if he could figure out the wall's message. Daniel listened to the king's promises, then prepared to reveal the meaning of the cryptic writing. Daniel said:

> [17] ...."Let your gifts be for yourself,
> and give your rewards to another;
> yet I will read the writing to the king,
> and make known to him the interpretation.
>
> (New King James Version, Daniel 5: 17)

Daniel started by reminding Belshazzar how God had blessed Nebuchadnezzar with a glorious kingdom, but due to his prideful heart and stubborn spirit, God stripped him of his fame and glory. The Lord eventually dethroned him and drove him to madness. Daniel emphasized that Belshazzar failed to learn humility from his grandfather's story. He then proceeded to interpret each word:

[26]...*Mene: God has numbered your kingdom, and finished it;*
[27] *Tekel: You have been weighed in the balances, and found wanting;*
[28] *Peres: Your kingdom has been divided, and given to the Medes and Persians."*

(New King James Version, Daniel 5:26-28*)*

While Belshazzar was busy feasting, the clever Persian Army ingeniously redirected the Euphrates River, which flowed beneath Babylon's wall, using tunnels and earth dams. The Babylonian soldiers were caught off guard and unable to defend themselves as the Persian forces managed to sneak under the walls and open the gates. Babylon was captured with ease, resulting in Belshazzar's demise. Upon returning to Babylon, Darius, his former governor, arrested Nabonidus.

[3] *Then I lifted my eyes and saw, and there, standing beside the river,*
was a ram which had two horns, and the two horns were high;
but one was higher than the other, and the higher one came up last.
[4] *I saw the ram pushing westward, northward, and southward, so that*
no animal could withstand him; nor was there any that could deliver
from his hand, but he did according to his will and became great.

(New King James Version, Daniel 8:3-4*)*

The dynamic Medo-Persians, Assyrians, Babylonians, and Scythians all had Indo-European roots and journeyed from Europe's hills to Asia's southwest corner, eventually venturing south towards Africa. Interestingly, Cyrus's grandfather held the title of the last Mede king. Nevertheless, Cyrus courageously rebelled against his grandfather, Astyages, ultimately uniting the Assyrians, Medes, and Persia into a formidable powerhouse. The Persians went on to conquer Lydia in 546 BC., and Babylon in 539 BC., eventually dominating most Greek villages along the Aegean Sea and Asia Minor.

Cyrus stood out among the Assyrians and Babylonians with his kind-hearted approach. He let the people he conquered follow their religion and didn't subject them to harsh treatment. Known as a generous leader, he allowed people to return to their native lands or stay within Persian territories. Cyrus showed immense appreciation for diverse religious beliefs, cultures, and ethnicities.

In Babylon, the Jewish community regarded Cyrus as a champion of freedom. As the first Aryan king to establish and advocate for human rights, Cyrus made significant strides in reforming society. During Assyrian and Babylonian celebrations, numerous women who refused to partake in lascivious activities suffered sexual assaults. However, Cyrus's introduction of a human rights charter eradicated such practices by enforcing strict discipline. Additionally, the charter abolished unpaid forced labor, much to the relief of many. The Jews particularly appreciated Cyrus's policy of allowing people to return to their homelands.

Before his passing, Isaiah assured the Israelites that God had blessed him with a prophecy about Cyrus's divine anointment for this unique mission in the following excerpt:

> [1] *Thus says the Lord to His anointed,*
> *To Cyrus, whose right hand I have held*
> *To subdue nations before him*
> *And loose the armor of kings,*

To open before him the double doors,
So that the gates will not be shut:
² 'I will go before you
And make the crooked places straight;
³ I will give you treasures of darkness
And hidden riches of secret places,
That you may know that I, the Lord,
Who call you by your name,
I Am the God of Israel.
⁴ For Jacob My servant's sake
And Israel My elect,
I have even called you by your name;
I have named you though you have not known Me.
⁵ I am the Lord, and there is no other;
There is no God besides Me.

(New King James Version, Isaiah 45:1-5*)*

After the death of Cyrus in battle, Cambyses II took over and marched his troops towards Egypt. The Egyptians, however, had employed Greek and Carian mercenaries to defend their land. Interestingly, many Greeks were already in Egypt, having been invited by Psammeticus I to ward off Assyria. Despite their fierce resistance against the Persian forces, the Egyptians suffered significant losses and were forced to retreat to Memphis. Cambyses followed them, and the Egyptians surrendered without fighting within the sacred temple. Thus, in 525 BC., Egypt became a part of the expanding Persian Empire.

Meanwhile, Cambyses dispatched spies to Ethiopia to present gifts to their king. Their real mission was to assess Ethiopia's strengths and weaknesses. However, the astute Ethiopian king saw through their deception and recognized them as Persian spies.

The king of Persians sent you not with these gifts because he much desired to become my sworn friend, nor is the account which ye give of yourselves valid, for ye have come to search out my kingdom. Also, your king is not a just man, for if was so, he had not coveted a land that is not his own nor brought slavery on a people who never did him any wrong.

> *Bear him this bow, and say, "The king of the Ethiopians thus advises the king of the Persians when the Persians can pull a bow of this strength thus easily, then let him thank the gods that they have not put it into the heart of the sons of the Ethiopians to covet countries which do not belong to them.*

(Herodotus, n.d.)

The spies returned to Cambyses, detailing the rare copper, gold, ivory, myrrh, and other treasures they had witnessed. They relayed the Ethiopian king's insult directed at Cambyses, who was enraged when his food was dubbed as dirt. Fueled by anger, Cambyses dispatched 50,000 men toward Ethiopia, torching the oracle of Zeus-Amun en route. Expeditions were also sent to Ammon and Carthage. However, their new Phoenician allies declined to mobilize their navy due to familial ties and oaths with the Carthaginians. Undeterred, they ventured deeper into the Ammon desert, where a sudden sandstorm engulfed them during lunch.

In the Ethiopian desert, Cambyses and his Persian soldiers were driven to desperation when their food supply ran out. They ate herbs and grass to survive but soon resorted to cannibalism as they pushed further into the barren landscape. Disturbed by the news of such gruesome acts, Cambyses retreated from Ethiopia without engaging in battle. Details of Cambyses's reign remain sparse except for accounts from select historians who label him an evil figure following Cyrus's demise.

Rumors abound that Cyrus married his sister and had his brother executed due to increasing popularity. His younger sister also met a violent end under his orders. Cyrus's desire for Egyptian dominion was stoked by his fascination with Egyptian women. This obsession continued with Cambyses, who took an Egyptian concubine while his soldiers enslaved Egyptian women as their concubines.

GREECE: FROM THE ANCIENT HELLENES TO ALEXANDER THE GREAT

The ancient Greeks, known as Hellenes, stemmed from a group of Aryans called the Sea People. These Indo-Europeans migrated from the Caspian Sea region to Crete, evolving from nomadic hunters and fierce warriors into skilled horse riders. They settled along the beautiful Aegean Sea. The first Aryan subgroup, the Dorians, found their home in Thessaly's plains, Peloponnesus, and Asia Minor. Conquering lands and burning villages paved the way for others to follow. The Greeks constructed oracular temples near volcanic craters to communicate with mystical entities. The Dorians ventured into Mycenae and Crete, devastating the local economy and suppressing non-Aryan cultures. One of these civilizations was the advanced Minoans of Crete, who thrived before the invasion.

Cretans originated from a mix of Israelites and Cushites before migrating to Crete's beautiful islands. Boasting Knossos, the Mediterranean's largest and most stunning city, as their capital, the Minoans constructed extravagant palaces adorned with exquisite murals depicting everyday life. Their expertise in sailing allowed them to engage in maritime trade across Spain, Egypt, North Africa, and beyond. The Minoans forged impressive trade partnerships across the Mediterranean, and their thriving commerce enabled them to construct magnificent palaces and amass a vast fortune. A sophisticated water system featuring interlinked aqueducts brought fresh water from afar directly into homes and public spaces. This advanced infrastructure not only supplied clean water but also included an underground drainage system.

The Minoans on the island of Crete were a peaceful society focused on harmony rather than conflict. Lacking defensive structures, they valued women's roles in leadership at a time when other cultures regarded women as mere possessions. Sadly, around 1500 BC., the thriving Minoan civilization faced near-destruction due to a volcanic eruption near Kalliste Island (now Santorini) and a massive tsunami. This natural disaster claimed almost 40,000 lives and left tsunamis towering up to 300 feet high to ravage their beautiful cities on seven small islands around Crete.

As if this calamity wasn't enough, the Minoans faced another devastating blow when the Aryans from the north invaded their lands soon after. The Aryans forced the surviving Minoans to retreat into the mountains while they seized control of Crete and developed it into an authoritative kingdom. Adopting the Minoans' shipbuilding expertise, these Balkan invaders transformed these maritime vessels into instruments of war, earning themselves the title of "Sea People."

The mighty Minoans faced a decline as they fled to the hills of the Karfi Mountains, leaving behind their once-glorious coastal cities. Overwhelmed by the Aryan invasion, many Minoans sought refuge in parts of Africa. The Aryans, guided by their deities, believed they had divine authority to conquer new lands. In the 12th century BC., a diverse group of Aryan invaders settled in southern Asia Minor, bringing Aeolians, Ionians, Sabines, and other Indo-European tribes. They embraced the eastern Aegean islands and absorbed the rich Minoan culture. The innovative Minoans had created impressive administrative buildings with massive columns, courtyards, and thriving trading systems. The Greeks recognized this genius and built prosperous colonies on Minoan foundations.

The Minoan legacy included charming paved streets, elegant mini-palaces adorned with hieroglyphic images, and advanced underground sewage systems. It's no wonder that much of Greco-Roman architecture was influenced by the exceptional engineering of the Minoans and Cushites.

By 338 BC., young Alexander the Great started his rise to power at just 18 years old. As King Philip's Macedonian cavalry commander at the Battle of Chaeronea, he played a crucial role in uniting Greek city-states with Asia Minor and the Aegean Islands under one powerful nation. Alexander ascended the throne two years later when his father fell victim to a bodyguard's betrayal. After King Philip's demise, Thebes rose in defiance. Alexander crushed the city and enslaved its people to quell further revolts. Determined to realize his father's vision, he set out to conquer Persia and merge the prosperous, ingenious western society with the eastern realm of Persia.

Alexander chose to fulfill his father's mission of invading Persia and merging the vibrant, affluent Western society with the Eastern realm of Persia. In 334 BC., he guided his 35,000-strong army across the Hellespont, catching Persian forces off guard near the Granicus River in Asia Minor and securing victory. As the Greeks reconstructed conquered lands, their artistic and technological prowess combined with the hardworking innovation of the East, forging unity. After conquering Syria, Alexander dispatched representatives to Jerusalem, urging the high priest to submit to Greece's mighty forces. However, Jewish elders refused this peace proposal. Undeterred, Alexander and his troops marched towards Jerusalem to make it a Grecian colony by force.

Upon reaching the city gates, High Priest Jaddua, adorned in his white robe with purple and gold accents, awaited alongside Jewish elders. When King Alexander spotted him, he removed his garments and bowed respectfully. Upon recognizing Jaddua from a divine dream, Alexander received prophecies of Greece's conquest of Persia. Similarly, Jaddua had been instructed in a plan to open the city gates for the king. Consequently, the Macedonians and Greeks retreated without conflict.

By 333 B.C., Alexander's army approached Issus on the Syrian coast, where Darius had fled. Striking at the Phoenician naval base of Tyre, Alexander eliminated Persian naval superiority with a relentless seven-month battle before successfully seizing the island. He constructed an impressive causeway connecting the island to the mainland using Lebanese cedar. Despite being outnumbered, Alexander's military genius shone through as he utilized cunning tactics, infantrymen, battering rams, artillery units, and mobile towers to secure victory.

In retaliation for their defiance, two thousand captives were executed while survivors were sold into slavery. In 332 BC., Alexander ventured across the Libyan Desert and along the Nile. He claimed Cushite territories close to Egypt and visited the oracle of Zeus-Ammon in Siwah Oasis. Advancing towards western Ethiopia after invading Upper Egypt's Kemet region, Alexander reconsidered upon witnessing the prowess of the Ethiopian Army. With Queen Candace poised for war atop her elephant, he steered his forces towards the coast without engaging in battle.

Moving on, Alexander's soldiers marched toward the Mediterranean Coast, conquering Ashleton and surrounding settlements. En route to southern Egypt, Alexander encountered

Persian soldiers in Gaza who tried to prevent his invasion. Utilizing his siege equipment, Alexander breached the fortress' thick walls, and fierce street combat ensued. Ultimately, Greece was victorious, and the Egyptians welcomed Alexander as their liberator from Persian rule, crowning him, Pharaoh.

Alexander built Alexandria's stunning and influential city on the Mediterranean coastline, a highlight of the ancient world. As he ventured through the Syrian Desert towards Persia, a face-off between Alexander and Darius occurred near Gaugamela and Arbela villages. During the Battle of Arbela, Persia's defeat led to Darius' demise at the hands of his soldiers during his escape attempt. Alexander quickly captured Babylon, preceded by Susa and the once-great city of Persepolis. Alexander's men took goods from royal residences and enormous storehouses stocked with gold and silver before setting fire to Darius' palace. Continuing his military campaigns for three more years, Alexander eventually returned to Babylon, where he fell ill with a fever and passed away at 32 years old in 323 BC.

Following Alexander's death, his four generals - known as the Diadochi - divided his vast kingdom as described in Daniel 8:22: "As for the broken horn and the four that stood up in its place, four kingdoms shall arise out of that nation, but not with its power."

5 And as I was considering, suddenly a male goat came from the west,
across the surface of the whole earth, without touching the ground;
and the goat had a notable horn between his eyes.
6 Then he came to the ram that had two horns,
which I had seen standing beside the river,
and ran at him with furious power.
7 And I saw him confronting the ram;
he was moved with rage against him, attacked the ram,

and broke his two horns. There was no power in the ram to withstand him,
but he cast him down to the ground and trampled him;
and there was no one that could deliver the ram from his hand.
⁸ Therefore the male goat grew very great; but when he became strong,
the large horn was broken, and in place of it four notable ones came up
toward the four winds of heaven.
⁹ And out of one of them came a little horn which grew exceedingly great
toward the south, toward the east, and toward the Glorious Land.

(New King James Version, Daniel 8:5-9*)*

Emerging from a humble agricultural Latin community within the Greek kingdom during the Bronze Age, Rome gradually expanded its territories across seven low, rolling hills. The Romans, Macedonians, and Greeks shared common roots as Indo-European peoples, all hailing from the mountainous regions of Europe. Nestled alongside the Tiber River on the Palatine and Esquiline hills, the Romans created larger settlements. While they absorbed elements of southern Greek cities' culture, their primarily agricultural lifestyle meant they mostly lived as farmers or shepherds in modest village huts. Rome began to flourish incredibly quickly, encompassing nearby Greek and Latin communities and growing its power across Italy. With this expansion came political and military control over neighboring cities. Around 509 BC., the Etruscan king Lucius Tarquinius was ousted, paving the way for a republic and granting citizens a say in their governance after eras of rule under seven different kings. While Greeks and Macedonians battled over land, Rome thrived in its internal growth throughout the empire.

Under Macedonian rule, the Romans created a government, trained their citizen-soldiers, and expanded their territory. All capable citizens had to serve in the military and supply their weapons, which sadly excluded the poorer class. Despite this limitation, Rome's strength grew as they defended their lands and eventually conquered the Italian peninsula. With the establishment of new laws to safeguard conquered societies, Rome gained more soldiers and prestige. They stationed troops in occupied territories to maintain security. Their conquests included the affluent colonies of Magna Graecia (Greater Greece), Campania, the Etruscans, and the mountain-dwelling Samnites south of Rome. It seemed as though the Romans aimed to impress their gods by amassing an extensive geographical domain to showcase their power.

In the third century BC., Rome and North African Carthage (Phoenicians) crossed paths as they traded along the Mediterranean Coast. The North African and Sicilian ports opened their gates to Roman traders, allowing Rome to delve deep into the heart of African civilization. While Carthage and Rome formed a trading alliance, Carthage couldn't help but worry about Rome's rising military prowess. For over a century, the Carthaginians and Greeks fiercely competed for control over the stunning and culturally diverse island of Sicily, which thrived as a center of Mediterranean trade. Sicily and Syracuse flourished as two of the world's most breathtaking and prosperous cities.

During the First Punic War, Greek rulers King Hiero II of Syracuse and Rome joined forces to dominate the islands of Sicily, Sardinia, and Syracuse. Despite their efforts, they couldn't seize complete control. This massive invasion ultimately resulted in Rome claiming Corsica from Carthage, establishing its first province outside the Italian Peninsula. The 20-year-long conflict took a heavy toll on Rome, claiming 100,000 lives and 700 warships. However, the Roman victory was nearly short-lived when Carthaginian General Hannibal Barca sought retribution for losing Sicily. Leading an ethnically diverse army, along with 37 elephants and a formidable cavalry, Hannibal crossed the treacherous French Alps to invade Italy.

Following the First Punic War, Rome set its sights on dismantling Carthage's hold on Spain and capturing Hannibal but ended up igniting the Second Punic War by attacking African territories they thought had been defeated already. Determined to counteract Carthaginian naval superiority, the Romans destroyed 500 Carthaginian warships and planned to isolate Hannibal's forces in Spain from their homeland. Undaunted, Hannibal resourcefully built enormous rafts to transport elephants and horses across the river. By 218 BC., Hannibal's forces stormed the Iberian city of Saguntum before marching onward through Gaul (Southern France). They swiftly captured supply convoys and emerged victorious against the Romans at Lake Trasimene and Trebia. The fierce battle at Cannae saw Hannibal's army decimate over 25,000 Roman soldiers and capture around 10,000 prisoners losing only 5,700 of their own. In 216 BC., Carthaginian forces prepared to confront a formidable Roman army of 80,000 strong.

As the Romans pushed into Hannibal's defenses, the Carthaginians cunningly encircled them and launched a surprise attack from behind. This strategic move led to the devastating loss of tens of thousands of Roman soldiers in a single day. Consequently, many citizens from Cannae, Capua, Syracuse, and Taranto revolted against Greco-Roman rule and sided with Hannibal.

In 213 BC., Hannibal set up camp outside Rome's walls after ravaging Italy. However, he had lost most of his siege engines and elephants. The Carthaginians were also dealt a heavy blow when an early snowstorm claimed the lives of nearly 30,000 troops. Using the remaining elephants to bulldoze walls and trample enemies, Hannibal continued his campaign on the back of the sole surviving elephant. Despite significant losses, Hannibal remained battle-ready with weapons and a powerful cavalry. The Roman legions were no match for him. Hannibal assumed his forces would be welcomed as liberators due to Rome's harsh rule, but most citizens remained loyal to their city.

Although Hannibal relentlessly tried to besiege cities like Capua, Taranto, and Syracuse, Carthage hesitated to send significant backup, worried about Rome's interception. After a daunting 15-year battle, Carthage's resources were running thin. Even though Hannibal attempted to break through the city walls and force the Romans to succumb to starvation, he was unsuccessful. Rome refused Hannibal's peace proposal, which included surrendering southern Italy, and several Romans faced execution for attempting to yield to the opposing side. Despite the grim situation, Romans maintained faith in their gods' protection until the end. This unyielding belief in divine intervention kept their spirits high. Meanwhile, Carthage's government chose not to send additional troops or supplies, focusing instead on defending Hispania and Sicily. At this point, Hannibal acknowledged that he couldn't defeat Rome without Carthage's support and called upon his brother Hasdrubal in Spain.

In 211 BC., a dramatic turn of events unfolded on the Spanish coast. Elder Cornelius Scipio and his brother Gnaeus faced an unfortunate demise while attempting to stop reinforcements from reaching Spain. Cornelius' adopted son, Publius Scipio Africanus, undeterred, took charge of the Roman army the following year, determined to endure the battle against Hamilcar Barca's mighty Spanish empire.

A triumphant moment it occurred when Publius Scipio Africanus defeated Hasdrubal Barca near the Ebro River at

Baecular. This led to the capture of Cartagena (Carthago Nova), a critical military stronghold in Hispania. Despite Hasdrubal's narrow escape with his remaining forces, he eventually united with Hannibal in Italy. In Rome, the Senate decided to burn all farms to prevent Hannibal's army from accessing resources. Scipio Africanus figured that the best way to defeat Hannibal was by attacking the Carthaginian territories in Africa. Rome made a pact with Saguntum to help them in southern Italy and fighting in Africa to assist their efforts.

Hannibal was forced to return to Africa to protect Carthaginian lands despite lacking reinforcements. In 202 BC., during the summer, Scipio Africanus led his troops to North Africa, where he outsmarted Hannibal at the Battle of Zama by using Hannibal's strategies against him. Despite many Roman leaders, like Senator Cato, wanting Publius Scipio Africanus to destroy everything in his path, he chose a more moderate approach. The Carthaginians had no choice but to surrender their navy, pay tribute to Rome, and relinquish all their foreign lands. Hannibal was permitted to step into a political role as a sign of mutual respect.

CHAPTER SEVEN

Ancient Rome and Carthage Heroes and Tragedies

Upon returning to Rome, the public hailed Scipio Africanus as a hero, although numerous politicians despised him for his devotion to the less fortunate. In his efforts to support small farmers, he proposed a bill to distribute land, which outraged the wealthy. Many of these farmers had transformed into citizen soldiers during wartime and were forced to sell their lands to powerful noble landowners after coming back from battle:

[24] *His power shall be mighty, but not by his own power;*
He shall destroy fearfully, And shall prosper and thrive;
He shall destroy the mighty, and also the holy people.
[25] *"Through his cunning*
He shall cause deceit to prosper under his rule;
And he shall exalt himself in his heart.

He shall destroy many in their prosperity.
He shall even rise against the Prince of princes;
But he shall be broken without human means.

(New King James Version, Daniel 8:24-25*)*

THE DESTRUCTION OF CARTHAGE AND THE THIRD PUNIC WAR

The Third Punic War erupted due to the Romans' greed and cunning tactics. Under the leadership of Hannibal, Carthage flourished as it excelled in agriculture and coastal trade. Hannibal purged the nation of corruption, and the Carthaginians transformed their land into an economic powerhouse. In exchange for peace, Carthage agreed to disarm its military and seek Rome's approval before taking action against neighboring territories. However, growing Roman influence forced Hannibal to escape to Syria, leaving Carthage vulnerable to raids from tribes like the Numidians.

Desperate for help, Carthage reached out to Rome for assistance but received only silence in return. Despite adhering to the treaty's terms by paying off their debts, Carthage was left at Rome's mercy. Rome eventually sent Senator Marcus Porcius Cato alongside a delegation to address the ongoing conflict. Astonished by Carthage's rapid recovery following the war, Cato grew wary of their newfound wealth and prosperity. Returning to Rome with the war on his mind, Senator Cato sought to persuade his fellow Romans that it was time for a decisive strike against Carthage. His notorious proclamation, "Carthage must be destroyed," echoed throughout countless speeches as he fought for his cause.

In 151 BC., Carthage bravely tried to prevent the Numidians, led by King Masinissa, from invading their lands. Rome saw this move as a treaty breach, and Cato pushed for war. By 149 BC.,

Rome waged war on Carthage, deploying 80,000 soldiers to seize the port of Utica near Carthage under Scipio Aemilianus' command. Faced with the threat of war, Carthage considered all possible options to appease Rome. Rome demanded 300 hostages from noble families and the surrender of all weapons. Carthage complied, handing over 200,000 armor sets and peacefully giving up Utica. But then, Cato shockingly told the Carthaginians to evacuate their coastal city and relocate inland to focus on agriculture; otherwise, their city would face heavy penalties. Realizing these demands would crush their nation and had already surrendered their weapons, Carthage found itself in dire straits.

Romans laid siege to the defenseless city, leading to a three-year standoff with many Carthaginians dying from hunger. In 146 BC., Roman forces finally broke through the city walls and launched a brutal attack that claimed over 600,000 lives. The elderly and ill were instantly killed, while any escape attempt resulted in decapitation or violent deaths for men, women, and children alike. The Romans fiercely attacked the city, setting it ablaze. They enslaved the residents and obliterated the Carthaginian library. Tragically, infants were cast into the raging fire, and women faced violations during this harrowing experience – all as retribution for not yielding. The nation found itself drowning in poverty and despair following the lengthy siege. Hannibal was held captive in Bithynia, and despite the king's orders to send him to Rome, he chose to end his life with poison. The Third Punic War erupted from a place of jealousy, ultimately obliterating most of Carthaginian history and its unique cultural identity.

[22] *I will turn My face from them, And they will defile My secret place; For robbers shall enter it and defile it.*

²³ 'Make a chain, For the land is filled with crimes of blood, And the city is full of violence.
²⁴ Therefore I will bring the worst of the Gentiles, And they will possess their houses;

(New King James Version, Ezekiel 7:22-23)

Nestled along the coast, Carthage, Israel's northern neighbor, was a bustling hub of trade and shipbuilding. This diverse region dominated the Mediterranean with its powerful navy and thriving commerce. The Carthaginians constructed impressive societies along the rocky shoreline, utilizing their lush landscapes and rich timber resources for various purposes. Their skilled artisans manufactured exquisite glassware, clothing, bronze and gold vessels, and items made from copper, lead, and ivory – their special dye being particularly sought after.

Unfortunately, the arrival of Anglo-Saxons from Canaan and Greek mercenaries introduced the worship of Baal, a deity that stirred great fury among the Carthaginians. As Roman forces approached their land, hundreds of Carthaginians engaged in the chilling practice of child sacrifice. They would place their firstborn sons in the fiery embrace of a giant statue of Baal, where scorching coals would devour them.

Once the Romans triumphed over Carthage, their gaze shifted eastward to the prosperous land of Corinth in Greece. They plundered the city, seizing its exquisite treasures as war spoils to bring back to Rome. Roman soldiers marched into Corinth, killing its men and enslaving its women and children, as described in Daniel 8:9.

Rome then turned its attention toward North Africa, focusing on their former ally, the Numidians (now northern Algeria). Here, Jugurtha rose to power, forming a close bond with Rome after befriending Scipio Aemilianus, the adopted grandson of Scipio Africanus during his time in Spain. Jugurtha even served alongside a Roman commander, Gaius Marius who later tasked with capturing him.

However, in 110 BC., Rome's invasion of Numidia wasn't successful – Jugurtha repelled them with great humiliation. Masterfully using the Libyan Desert for cover, he bewildered Roman soldiers and made their leaders appear incompetent. Jugurtha's prowess earned the admiration of several Roman politicians; many were even accused of accepting bribes and engaging in corruption.

Facing a lack of skilled warriors, Gaius Marius boldly formed a volunteer army that attracted lower-class citizens by eliminating property requirements for soldier enlistment. In the early days, Roman soldiers were primarily unpaid farmers, only reaping the rewards of their conquests. To thrive and persist, the military need full-time devoted personnel, improved protection equipment, and an unwaveringly loyal army.

In 107 BC., Roman forces managed to subdue Numidia by splitting the land but, unfortunately, didn't capture Jugurtha. It wasn't until 104 BC., that Jugurtha was finally captured due to a betrayal by the Mauretanian ruler and handed over to Sulla, the Roman legion's leader. Paraded through the streets in chains and royal attire, Jugurtha met a grim end, locked in a cell and left to die of starvation. Soon after, Rome expanded its territories by incorporating Mauretania and Numidia's coastal regions.

By 31 BC., Octavian emerged victorious from the pivotal Battle of Actium off the coast of Greece. The climactic final battle occurred in Northeast Africa against Mark Antony and Egypt's Queen Cleopatra during the Roman Civil War. Following Julius Caesar's assassination, Rome was divided into three major factions. Caesar's great-nephew emerged as the primary heir and established a ruling trio, the Second Triumvirate.

However, the romantic entanglement between Antony and Cleopatra created tensions within this trio, eventually escalating into a civil war when the Senate declared war on Cleopatra. Roman general Marcus Aemilius Lepidus was ousted from the Triumvirate, steering Rome on an entirely new course. Mark Anthony, father to three children with Cleopatra, was declared a traitor. He escaped to Egypt alongside his lover, with Octavian hunting them down. Their dramatic love story and the civil war ended when Mark Anthony took his own life with his sword, collapsing into Cleopatra's embrace, as blood stained her clothes.

Cleopatra's army, commanded by Mark Antony's fleet, gave in to Octavian without any resistance. In Alexandria, she was allowed to choose her destiny. As per Strabo's account, Cleopatra opted for suicide – either with a toxic ointment or an Egyptian cobra's venom. Her political foe emerged triumphant, clearing his way toward becoming the Emperor of the Roman Empire. Egypt's riches were then absorbed into the Ptolemaic Kingdom, significantly boosting Rome's wealth. Egypt was the most affluent region of the Italian Peninsula, with Alexandria being a major port city and economic center in the Mediterranean and Red Sea Coast. Rome benefited greatly from an array of grains, nuts, and olive oil supplied by Egypt's coastal regions throughout the year.

In 25 BC., Aelius Gallus, Egypt's prefect or chief magistrate, initiated a military campaign against the Cushites. He destroyed Napata, pushed their borders further south, and breached a border agreement. The region was abundant in gold, silver, ivory, and various precious minerals. The Romans attempted to tax Ethiopia and establish a new border. Aelius Gallus led a sizeable armed force into Meroe. However, Queen Candace repelled the Roman army of 30,000 troops that attempted to march toward Meroe. Strabo states that Queen Amanirenas and her Kushite army seized all of Syene and the Triacontaschoinos (the borderland between Meroe and Philae) while demolishing Roman statues at Philae. The Kushite soldiers attacked the Roman garrison so fiercely that Aelius Gallus took his own life out of disgrace.

> [6]*For Unto us a child is born*
> *Unto us a Son is given*
> *And the government will be upon*
> *His shoulder.*
> *And His name will be called*
> *Wonderful, Counselor, Mighty God,*
> *Everlasting Father, Prince of Peace.*
> [7]*Of the increase of His government*
> *There will be no end...*
>
> *(New King James Version,* Isaiah 9:6-7*)*

Yeshua Ha'Mashiach, also known as Jesus Christ in English, was born in Bethlehem, Palestine, just south of Jerusalem. His humble beginning occurred in a manger, a simple animal feeding trough. From the moment he was born, he faced dangers and death threats, causing the young dark-skinned Palestinian child to flee his homeland and head towards Northeast Africa. Finding refuge in Southern Egypt, he narrowly escaped a dreadful decree targeting young boys two years old and under. This slaughter in Bethlehem highlighted the frightening reality for Black infants at the time. However, amidst the chaos, Egypt served as a sanctuary for Yeshua during his early life. As a result, Egypt became one of the first nations to host Christians. This

North African nation is now home to Coptic Christians - an ancient denomination still prevails among a small percentage of Egypt's population.

During His time on Earth, Jesus Christ was known as "Yeshua," meaning "Salvation." He carried the title of Messiah (Ha'Mashiach) or "Anointed One," signifying His role as the Savior of the world and servant of YHVH, also called "Yahweh." In Islamic tradition, Jesus Christ is called Isa ibn Maryam or Jesus, son of Mary. As a prophet and messenger of Allah (God), He was entrusted to guide the Children of Israel. In Hinduism, the enigmatic and Supreme God among all deities is Brahma. Brahma reigns supreme, possessing boundless power and radiating with the brilliance of thousands of suns.

Brahma possesses boundless strength and radiates with the intensity of thousands of suns. As an all-powerful and all-knowing being, he represents the ultimate spiritual reality and is the creator of everything, including fallen and non-fallen angels. His magnificent glory has no equal, illuminating and delighting all, from whom everything emerges, sustains life upon birth, and eventually returns.

Fascinatingly, the ancient Aryans, originating from the Balkans and authors of the Vedas (Aryan Bible), connected Brahma with the timeless deities of Shudra, Dasas, and Panis – India's indigenous people. Interestingly, India's native population primarily comprised Black individuals who migrated from Africa. The Aryans regarded Brahma as a mysterious god associated with India's indigenous community.

THE LIFE AND TEACHINGS OF JESUS CHRIST IN PALESTINE

In the midst of fierce resistance against the Roman Empire, the story of Yeshua Ha'Mashiach unfolded. It all began in 63 BC., when Roman General Pompey stepped in to resolve a conflict between Syrians and Jews, which led to both sides surrendering. This turbulent history can be traced back even further to 164 BC., when a priest named Mattathias ignited a rebellion by killing a Syrian commissioner, who insisted on a sacrifice to Zeus. The Maccabee family ruled Judea until Pompey seized control in 63 BC., appointing Hyrcanus II as high priest after significant Jewish losses.

Fast forwarding to 40 BC., Augustus Caesar designated Herod as Judea's procurator. Driven by suspicions of infidelity, Herod executed his wife Mariamme, who was also Hyrcanus' daughter. Her sons, Alexander and Aristobulus, sought revenge for their mother's death by conspiring against their father; however, their plans were foiled and they were executed. Determined to eliminate Yeshua the Christ, Herod ordered the execution of all male children in Bethlehem and its surrounding areas – an act that ultimately fulfilled Jeremiah's prophecy.

> [18]*"A voice is heard in Ramah,*
> *weeping and great mourning,*
> *Rachel weeping for her children,*
> *And refusing to be comforted,*
> *because they are no more."*
>
> (*New King James Version,* Matthew 2:18)

In the Bible, prophets often acted as advisers to kings. As per Cushite tradition, Moses became an Ethiopian Army general after fleeing from the pharaoh and living in Midian. Nehemiah, another prophet, climbed the ranks in the Persian military and was assigned by King Cyrus of Persia to establish a Jewish homeland. He rode into Jerusalem with a powerful escort, unlike Jesus, the Son of God, who entered on a donkey and shared divine teachings with the poor while healing and comforting those in need.

The Romans gained control over Palestine during that period, causing divisions among Jewish communities. Jesus grew up in Nazareth, a small village located in the Galilee region which experienced harsh oppression. As he got older, Jesus became an advocate for disadvantaged people; however, many Hebrews embraced an unjust caste system that rewarded compliance.

Jesus introduced a movement focused on salvation and balance, threatening the wealth of affluent Gentiles and Hebrews alike. This equilibrium movement sought to unveil the dark aspects of this corrupt caste system or a structure based on supremacy to offer people a choice between good or embracing a corrupt system.

Yeshua Ha'Mashiach, a dark-skinned Palestinian Jew, was invited to minister at the Capernaum Synagogue in Nazareth, where he had lived as a young child. With its artistic beauty and high-ranking Roman officials, the city was called the Galilee of the Gentiles, bringing truth to Isaiah's prophecy, "The people who walk in darkness have seen a great light."

He was handed the book of the prophet Isaiah and found where it was written:

> *[1] The spirit of the Lord God is upon me,*
> *because the Lord has anointed me;*
> *he has sent me to bring good news to the oppressed,*
> *to bind up the brokenhearted, to proclaim liberty to the captives,*
> *and release to the prisoners;*
> *[2] to proclaim the year of the Lord's favor,*
> *and the day of vengeance of our God;*
>
> *(New Revised Standard, Isaiah 61:1-2)*

As he captured the audience's full attention, he declared, "Today, this Scripture has come to life in your presence." Yeshua then closed the book, returned it to the attendant, and took his seat.

In this period, a gathering of Gentiles was unique. Jews, a minority in Israel, faced both physical and mental subjugation. Although Gentiles ruled most of Israel, they still absorbed various aspects of nearby cultures while maintaining their Eurocentric way of living. Once, a graceful crowd was slow to understand the importance of a brief sermon. The people soon questioned the authenticity of the message. The book of Luke is written, "All were amazed by His demeanor and the eloquent words that flowed from His lips," yet they asked, "Isn't this Joseph's son?" At that precise moment, Yeshua rose to deliver a powerful oration in the synagogue, touching the depths of the congregants' souls and warning them against worshipping at the altar of whiteness. A new movement was emerging, promoting love and equality for all. Yeshua's words angered the congregation and those Israelites who had compromised their beliefs to obtain a higher status in Roman-controlled society.

Yeshua seized the opportunity to call out their wrongdoings, taking the audience by surprise. He cleverly taught them a lesson from history, which the worshipers weren't fond of. Their dissatisfaction quickly escalated into fury. Unfazed, Yeshua Ha'Mashiach carried on with his message, saying:

But I tell you truly, many widows were in Israel in the days of Elijah when the heaven was shut up three years and six months, and there was a great famine throughout all the land; but to none of them was Elijah sent except to Zerephath, in the region of Sidon, to a woman who was a widow. And many lepers were in Israel in the time of Elisha the prophet, and none of them was cleaned except Naaman the Syrian.

²⁹ They rose up, dragged Jesus out of town, and took him to the top of the hill on which their town was built. They meant to throw him over the cliff, ³⁰ but he walked through the middle of the crowd and went his way.

(Good News Translation, Luke 4:29-30*)*

Many think that God made the people blind, allowing Yeshua the Christ to flee. Some say Yeshua faced the angry crowd and bravely walked straight toward them. The Jews worried that his fame would trigger Roman anger, but they were ready to fight against the cruel system. Yeshua's mission as the Messiah was to free humanity—including the aggressive Balkan settlers known as Aryan Gentiles. Thanks to divine grace, he aimed to break their caste-based control over the Israelites' lives. With the world becoming stranger by the day, categorizing people by their physical features was no longer acceptable in this era of Salvation.

Yeshua guided his followers down a different path, encouraging them to shun violence and embrace goodness: "Pursue virtue instead of evil, so that you may prosper and enjoy the Lord's presence, the God of hosts." Yeshua referred to the story of Naaman during a synagogue gathering, depicting a connection where leprosy was considered less significant. Naaman was serving as an enslaved to Ben-Hadad, King of Syria, according to the second Book of Kings, chapter 18. Both Naaman and his master bowed in reverence at the Temple of Rimmon during their worship. Although Naaman lived in a Pagan land, the Lord punished him with leprosy for serving a foreign god. Miraculously, the Lord later healed Naaman of the disease.

However, neither Gehazi's family nor other lepers were granted the same mercy. "Therefore, the leprosy of Naaman shall cling to you and your descendants forever. And he went out from his presence leprous, as white as snow" (2 Kings 5:27).

The Almighty Universal Father revealed Himself through Yeshua Ha'Mashiach, extending salvation and redemption to all people, not just the Hebrews. Yeshua had a divine mission with a message of love and gospel meant for every willing ear.

Yeshua the Christ's capture, is a turning point in Christianity, as documented in the canonical gospels. After his famous Last Supper and Judas' treacherous kiss, Jesus was captured, inciting mixed feelings among the Jews. Some appreciated his peaceful ways, while others struggled to balance their faith with Roman rule. Pontius Pilate, the Judean governor, gave the people a choice: free Jesus or the notorious thief Barabbas. In the end, they chose to release Barabbas.

In the heart of the Roman Empire, Paul, an exemplary apostle, spent his days traveling far and wide, even to the fascinating land of Greece. Born in Jerusalem, Paul held Roman citizenship and was a driving force behind the growth of Christianity across Rome. Imagine stepping foot in Corinth during the first century, a diverse city buzzing with half a million people! That's precisely where Paul resided for an impressive 18 months.

The Corinth Church was a thriving melting pot, home to individuals from Greece, Rome, Egypt, and indigenous Cretan communities. As seekers of better economic opportunities, these diverse people united under the common goal of spiritual growth. It was within this lively atmosphere that Paul rubbed shoulders with Titius Justus, Aquila, Priscilla, and Lydia - kind-hearted individuals who supported his missionary work financially. And amid the breathtaking backdrop of the Aegean Sea, he penned his most significant masterpiece - the Epistle of Romans.

Paul, joined by the historian Luke, journeyed to spread the word of God. Luke, the only non-Jewish author in the Bible, penned two parts of the New Testament—the Gospel of Luke and Acts of the Apostles. Paul directed his letters toward Jews and Christians, warning against their Pagan ways and sharing plans to visit Rome, Jerusalem, and Spain. Confronting Elymas, a deceitful sorcerer seeking to mislead believers, Paul struck him blind as punishment for his blasphemy. Afterward, he settled in Ephesus and shared the gospel throughout Asia Minor for three years. Sadly, in 68 A.D., following his fifth missionary expedition, Paul was beheaded outside Rome during Emperor Nero's rule—dying a martyr's death.

"And the fourth kingdom shall be as strong as iron, since iron breaks in pieces and shatters everything; and like iron that crushes, that kingdom will break in pieces and crush all the others" (Daniel 2:40).

The Western Roman Empire comprised western provinces characterized by powerful imperial courts and a strong Latin culture. When Octavian triumphed, he played a crucial role in merging the Greek civilization from the East with the Roman provinces of the West. This paved the way for a united Roman Empire seeking to move past its ancient Pagan roots. In this diverse realm, Africans and Jews reached prominent ranks and contributed significantly to Rome's religious landscape.

Even before the Apostle Paul's arrival, Romans had been introduced to the concept of a singular divine force governing nature. This sparked a transformation in their traditional belief system, gradually morphing the cults of various deities into one that recognized a single God. On another note, historians like Tacitus and Pytheas described Germanic and Scythian tribes living east of the Rhine River who worshiped Nerthus, a fertility goddess and earth mother figure. Interestingly enough, her influence was also felt in Roman religious practices. Many members of these Germanic tribes served as soldiers within the Roman military.

The Roman slave system is infamous for its brutality, fueled by a constant demand for cheap labor from Rome and its wars. Coastal Africa became a hunting ground for raiders and pirates, who targeted helpless children and war prisoners. These enslaved individuals were provided to affluent landowners for various farming, mining, construction, and public projects. Enslaved people were auctioned off based on their unique abilities after being stripped naked to be thoroughly inspected by potential buyers.

Predominantly comprised of captured Africans, the slave population also included prisoners of war from Germany, Russia, and Spain. Slavery played a crucial role in Rome's economic growth and social fabric. In mining, enslaved people faced particularly harsh conditions, with many sufferings' extreme cruelty and perishing under the strain of their labor. Conversely, enslaved people in military service held a certain status and privileges. However, enslaved men perceived as threats were subject to castration. Enslaved women often found themselves forced into roles such as domestic servants, cooks, housekeepers, or sex workers.

Disobedient enslaved people bore the brunt of severe punishments like being shackled together. Those who revolted or attempted to escape faced crucifixion or being burned alive. In 71 BC., after the failed insurgence led by Spartacus against Rome, 6,000 renegades enslaved people were crucified along the road from Capua to Rome as a chilling message. Conversely, numerous leaders implemented laws to shield enslaved people from mistreatment and harsh punishment. In 212 A.D., all inhabitants of the Roman Empire were granted citizenship, giving them the freedom to practice their religion openly. The economy heavily relied on slave labor, with enslaved people taking up positions as teachers, architects, skilled workers, and doctors. Many were set free in exchange for their unwavering dedication at their owner's request.

As the number of enslaved people grew, so did the seeds of rebellion. With many enslaved individuals conscripted or liberated serving in the military, they held significant sway when revolts arose. Some even purchased freedom for themselves and their families, climbing the social and economic ladder and unsettling Rome's upper class. Numerous Africans ascended to government positions during this time, including emperors like Septimius Severus – commander of the Danubian legions who presided over both eastern and western Roman territories for 17 years. Severus enacted political and military changes, replacing the Praetorian Guard with fresh military legions and auxiliary reserve squads led by proficient field leaders rather than senatorial diplomats. Consequently, Italy's nobility lost much of its power, while the Roman Senate diminished rapidly under Severus's rule. These additional troops significantly bolstered local security and diversified Rome's combat tactics while reinforcing provincial defense.

Born in the Roman colony of Leptis Magna in western Libya, Septimius Severus was Rome's first African emperor. He entered Rome unopposed after soldiers declared him emperor and ended Emperor Julianus Severus by executing him along with 29 senators. Despite his mixed-race heritage, Julianus Severus treated Africans and Jewish people harshly. His mother was of African descent but was born in Rome. Septimius Severus hailed from a long line of Punic aristocrats who had advanced to senatorial ranks within Rome, wielding both military and judicial power.

[11] ...."*Ask Me of things to come concerning My sons; And concerning the work of My hands,...*

[14] *Thus says the Lord: "The labor of Egypt and merchandise of Cush And of the Sabeans, men of stature, Shall come over to you, and they shall be yours; They shall walk behind you, They shall come over in chains; And they shall bow down to you...*

[16] *They shall be ashamed And also disgraced, all of them; They shall go in confusion together...*

(New King James Version, Isaiah 45:13-16*)*

CHAPTER EIGHT

From Biblical Curses to Imperial Exploitation: The African and American Saga

C ain cruelly killed his brother Abel in a gripping story from the Bible. As Adam and Eve's firstborn son, Cain followed in his father's footsteps as a farmer. Meanwhile, his younger sibling, Abel, became a wandering shepherd, tending to his flock. Intriguingly, the Lord favored Abel's offering of a young sheep over Cain's sheaf of grain due to Cain's lack of faith and preparation. According to the laws in Leviticus, a proper grain offering demands fine wheat flour accompanied by olive oil and frankincense. In the fascinating tradition of ancient Hebrews under Mosaic Law, the High Priest performed an annual atonement ritual for the people's sins on the Day of Atonement or Yom Kipper. This significant ceremony involved the fates of two goats: one to be sacrificed as a blood offering for sin redemption and reconciliation with

God. At the same time, the other - known as the scapegoat - would be sent off into the wilderness bearing the burden of their collective sins, never to return.

Cain, once a skilled farmer, faced the harsh consequence of losing his farming abilities after committing the heinous act of killing his brother Abel, a shepherd. In the biblical account of Genesis, God cursed Cain: "Now you are under a curse and driven from the ground, which opened its mouth to receive your brother's blood from your hand. When you work the ground, it will no longer yield its crops for you." Stripped of melanin and plagued by an incurable skin disease, Cain was forced to wander the land of Nod.

THE DEVASTATING CONSEQUENCES OF EUROPEAN COLONIZATION

As time passed, Cain's descendants roamed the freezing wilderness opposite the Balkans, ever searching for sustenance. Although descendants of Cain - or anyone banished to the Caucasus Mountains and Old Europe's Balkans (before they migrated to Ancient Crete and Roman territory) - had acclimatized to their environment, these rugged hills offered no mercy. However, they were skillfully adapted for hunting and warfare, as their mastery of capturing animals enabled them to unite seamlessly. They could easily kill prey and move swiftly on a moment's notice.

The wandering lifestyle empowered them to pursue sustenance and conquer foreign lands. They had to adapt to the harsh, cold environment and sharpen their hunting and tracking skills. This combative way of life transformed the relationship between the exiled inhabitants of the Balkans and the prosperous, dark-skinned farmers to the south. As time passed, the nomadic tribes, fueled by envy and a desire for retribution, returned to the Afrocentric world to torment, eliminate, or enslave those they once saw as foes.

The Hebrew-speaking people have long been considered the "first fruit" in evolutionary terms, developing a special bond with God as the initial offspring of humanity. Lepers and descendants of Cain were deemed impure and left to wander the earth without a cure. To truly comprehend God's silence and reluctance to meddle in human affairs, we must delve into the depths of history.

The early inhabitants of the Balkans fell under the influence of sinister forces, spreading a malicious affliction that seeped into Hebrew culture like a poisonous, unseen mist. Those cast out because of Cain's lineage wandered the frigid world, unable to profit from the land until the Messiah's salvation lifted their curse. In essence, God's firstborn focused more on aiding and educating their foes than honoring their connection to God, underestimating their own freedom's worth. Balancing unwavering devotion to God with an all-out struggle for dominance was unfamiliar to them. The Bible tells us that Abel's heart aligned with God while Cain's did not.

Throughout history, Hebrew men often fell victim to migrating settlers from the Balkans. These invaders employed a divide-and-conquer strategy, targeting Hebrews who didn't submit—those who resisted faced enslavement or brutal death. Freedom eluded the earliest members of humanity's family as they endured ongoing attempts to dehumanize them. Meanwhile, captured women faced assimilation into the invaders' world as concubines, subjected to extreme humiliation.

* * *

After the fall of the Roman Empire, international trade among its former territories dwindled. The Romans had heavily relied on their conquests to support their empire, and the decline in trade decreased the demand for enslaved people. During this historical period, Europe was in a depression. In 1415, Portugal's Prince Henry sent envoys to explore Africa's wealth, leading to the capture of Ceuta—a Moorish port city in North Africa. The Romans knew about Africa long before their empire fell since much of their food originated from the African coast. North Africa was a key supplier of grains and olive oil for trade and tax revenue after the Roman Empire annexed places like Carthage and Egypt. They imported grain from Egypt and other goods from Africa and Asia via camels and ships.

As the Portuguese ventured into Africa, they began trading along Ghana's West African coast, also known as the Gold Coast, which Black Africans predominantly inhabited. Ghana was a thriving agricultural society with vast resources and an advanced trade system. The coastal region presented excellent export opportunities, benefiting Europe's economy due to Ghana's advanced civilization. Though the Roman Empire had previously traded with Western Africa for valuable metals and agricultural goods, its collapse led to individual states struggling for survival. The Portuguese were the first Europeans to venture into Africa following the end of the Middle Ages and the decline of the Roman Empire. They were eagerly welcomed by Africans interested in trading with them and even allowed to construct temporary mud shelters. While this paved the way for Portugal to establish a thriving trade system that could rejuvenate European markets, their intentions were darker than any African ruler or commoner could have anticipated.

The Portuguese were exposed to a variety of crops grown in Africa, including coconuts, pineapples, figs, lemons, corn, cucumbers, beans, peas, bananas, lettuce, rice, peanuts, kola nuts, sweet potatoes, wheat, turnips, barley, garlic, onions, sesame, mangoes, watermelons, sugarcane, and numerous spices. Sugar sparked a need for cheap labor, creating a booming slave trade that boosted the African and American economies. This newfound wealth appeared to justify using enslaved people to support Europe's increasing demand for food and higher living standards. The Portuguese king urged African chiefs to provide them with enslaved people, fueling a rapid rise in hatred and relentless greed. Portugal and the remnants of the Roman Empire now had the means to feed their growing populations.

The kidnapping of Africans for slave labor soon began along the coast, as countless individuals were torn from their families and loaded onto ships bound for Europe. With their families shattered, Africans sought solace in their tribes, prioritizing self-preservation amidst mistrust and fear between neighboring groups. The mere mention of Europeans instilled terror in their hearts. Europeans erected forts and trading posts along Africa's coast to facilitate the collection and transport of enslaved people. Within these fortifications, precious commodities like gold, sugarcane, cotton, and tobacco were exchanged. Europeans even established slave colonies on Cape Verde and Sao Tome islands to boost sugar production, leading to an influx of settlers. When African rulers failed to supply enough enslaved people, Europeans turned to Arab traders or Moorish pirates to fill the gap. The Arabs, influenced by perceived social hierarchies and following Europe's ruthless footsteps, willingly participated in this cruel enterprise.

The Arabs, with their mixed European and African heritage, believed their lighter skin made them superior to dark-skinned Africans, who were considered primitive and akin to their European oppressors. Avoiding those who wished to rob Africans of their freedom became more difficult as smuggling emerged as a cunning tactic from the white man's strategy book. Arab traders and the Portuguese cooperated due to the former's knowledge of the land and the languages spoken by their captives. Their Islamic faith was ignored as long as it benefited white imperialism. Sadly, this caused little sympathy for the European invaders bent on spreading white supremacy across Africa. The oppressors exploited ethnic and tribal divisions to fuel conflict between tribes. Sacred trust played a crucial role in fostering these divisions, leading tribes toward destruction or enslavement. The ultimate goal was to disrupt peace and sow hatred between tribes, preventing a united defense.

The Arabs befriended Africans on behalf of the Europeans, who patiently awaited near the shoreline for their soon-to-be-enslaved prisoners. The Arabs sometimes attacked villages at night or dusk, causing chaos among residents. As villagers fled in fear, they were captured and shackled. These prisoners were marched for miles through dense jungles, bound together with iron chains and bamboo yokes, before being given over to Europeans to be sold as enslaved people.

[64] *"Then the Lord will scatter you among all peoples,*

from one end of the earth to the other,

and there you shall serve other gods,

which neither you nor your fathers have known—wood and stone.

[65] *And among those nations you shall find no rest, nor shall the sole of your foot have a resting place; but there the Lord will give you a trembling heart,*

failing eyes, and anguish of soul.

[66] *Your life shall hang in doubt before you; you shall fear day and night, and have no assurance of life.*

(New King James Version, Deuteronomy 28:64-66)

In 1492, representing the Spanish monarchy, Christopher Columbus embarked on a journey for geographical discovery.

As an experienced sailor, he had previously worked with the Portuguese merchant service and ventured to Africa. He expanded his astronomy, cartography, and geometry knowledge at the University of Pavia. Setting sail from Spain, Columbus aimed to discover India and the prosperous Spice Islands of Southeast Asia. However, powerful eastward winds blew his ship off course, leading him to wreck off Hispaniola's coast in the western Atlantic Ocean. Upon arrival, the natives offered Columbus vast regions of land and helped establish a settlement known as La Navidad in modern-day Haiti. Due to their unsuccessful journey to India, the settlers called these inhabitants "Indians."

During Columbus's first visit to the Americas, he observed the indigenous people smoking dried tobacco leaves. The locals welcomed him warmly and were even open to sharing their land. However, tensions arose between the settlers and Anacaona, a Taino princess who became queen after her husband Caonabo's death. The European settlers bargained for food and goods from the natives as a tribute to the Spanish Crown. 1493 upon returning from his second voyage, Columbus discovered that all 39 settlers had been killed and their settlements destroyed. To justify these terrible acts, natives from America and indigenous Africans were labeled as barbarians, animalistic rapists, and treated like predators.

The local Indigenous people fought against Spanish rule by refusing to pay tribute and follow their rules. During a feast with Queen Anacaona and her followers, Columbus, supported by his armed cavalry, set fire to the residence and executed those accused of conspiracy. Sadly, Queen Anacaona was arrested and hanged before her people at the young age of 29. Columbus established new settlements on the island's eastern side, naming one of them La Isabela in 1493, now known as the Dominican Republic. He also founded a settlement at Yaguana near today's

Leogane in 1502. As news of riches discovered in these lands spread across Europe, settlers were lured by offers of free land.

King Ferdinand and Queen Isabella permitted Europeans to settle in the Americas under their protection to support this colonization. This caused many Natives to flee their homes and seek shelter in the jungle. In turn, European explorers freely roamed the unoccupied islands along the northern and western coast of the Atlantic, searching for gold and other valuable treasures. To safeguard their New World interests, Portugal and Spain signed a treaty dividing control over Atlantic routes; Portugal managed the South Atlantic around Africa, while Spain held sway over North Atlantic routes leading to the Americas. Unfortunately, similar to Africa, what began as a warm welcome from indigenous inhabitants eventually turned into a devastating reality for them.

Spain colonized the Americas, setting up schools, hospitals, and plantations based on a capitalist economic system. The Indigenous people were subjected to forced labor and indoctrination by Catholic missionaries who sought to convert them to European Christianity. Consequently, entire native villages and communities vanished as they faced relocation, oppression, and cruelty – all to reshape Europe's economy. The soldiers diligently trained massive canines to hunt, protect, and fiercely assault Indigenous people. Demanding tributes of gold, copper, brass, or agricultural products from Indigenous leaders, the Spanish Sovereign ensured that any resistance was met with severe mutilations for intimidation.

Within half a century, the European invaders annihilated nearly 4 million members of the Taino community, part of the Arawakan-speaking natives. Populations across the Caribbean and American mainland witnessed merciless deaths by weaponry, canine attacks, or fatal diseases like swine flu – brought on by European settlers and foreign livestock. The Indigenous people had no natural defenses against these infections. Moreover, countless natives faced death due to extreme hunger as Europeans seized their farmlands. Others succumbed to exhaustion working in mines. Survivors were compelled to embrace the Catholic Church's dominance and forfeit their traditional beliefs. Those who refused had no choice but to submit or suffer the painful consequences of deprivation.

⁴ So they worshiped the dragon who gave authority to the beast;
and they worshiped the beast, saying,
"Who is like the beast? Who is able to make war with him?"
¹⁵ He was granted power to give breath to the image of the beast, that
the image of the beast should both speak and cause as many as would not
worship the image of the beast to be killed.
(New King James Version, Revelation 13:4,15)

The discovery of the Americas sparked a soaring demand for enslaved people, particularly after the Native population was decimated by genocide, famine, and disease. This led to the mass importation of enslaved Africans who primarily hailed from West Africa. Thousands were brought to work on farms for their white masters, tending to crops like tobacco, cotton, coffee, cocoa, corn, beans, peanuts, and sweet potatoes. In addition to tending the fields', enslaved Africans were also burdened with domestic chores in their captors' homes. Forced to adapt to the ways of the white man, they cooked meals and cleaned toilets and laundry. African and Native societies saw their way of life drastically altered upon encountering the white race. Fearful of kidnapping, many began residing in smaller villages.

The rich resources found in Africa and the Americas fueled an exploitative cycle that placed blame on the victims of imperialism, colonization, and white supremacy. Bountiful fertile lands led to thriving agriculture and timber industries – sugar cane plantations, cattle ranches, and mining businesses flourished. European nations combatted fiercely over these resources – with the Roman Catholic Church serving as a mediator in matters involving African wealth and access to America's resources. By 1625, French settlements sprouted on Tortuga Island and the mainland. The English and Dutch soon followed suit, greedily seizing land from Indigenous people for their gain – competing for dominance along the coastlines.

In 1655, Great Britain seized Jamaica and relocated its people to Port Royal, a bustling port city in the southeast that attracted English, Dutch, and French pirates. These three nations aimed to disrupt Spain's longstanding monopoly in the West Indies, turning the region into a fierce battleground. The British and French partnership emerged in 1657 to challenge Spain's dominance over the West Indies territories, ultimately gaining control of present-day Haiti. The Treaty of Basle saw Spain relinquish the western part of Hispaniola to France, then renamed Saint-Domingue. By 1697, Hispaniola was split between French and Spanish rule.

Many native inhabitants fled to the mountains to escape the horrors inflicted by European settlers. In 1762, the British claimed Havana, Cuba; however, a peace treaty between Spain and France in 1763 exchanged British control of Florida and the Bahamian islands for Cuba. A one-armed enslaved person from Africa named MacKandal escaped in 1751 and formed a group of maroons to rebel against white settlers in Saint Domingue. Together with his alliance, MacKandal devised a plan to poison plantation owners' drinking water using poisons crafted from local herbs.

The group skillfully executed nighttime raids on plantations, setting properties ablaze and poisoning households. Over 6,000 fatalities occurred before MacKandal's eventual betrayal by a tortured enslaved woman who confessed his actions. Captured at last, MacKandal met his end when he was burned alive in Cap-Francias' public square. In 1792, Leger-Felicite Sonthonax embarked on a mission the French Legislative Assembly assigned to calm the raging slave revolt on Hispaniola Island. However, his efforts were in vain. Meanwhile, the United States gained independence from Britain in 1776, inspiring wealthy white residents on Hispaniola to seek a similar liberation from France.

Napoleon Bonaparte commanded his brother-in-law, General Charles Leclerc, to lead a 20,000-strong army and warship fleet to quell the rebellion in 1802. They joined forces with white colonists and accessible mixed-race military units led by Alexandre Pétion to restore the brutal system of slavery. Pétion was a product of French and African heritage trained in France. Many mixed-race soldiers sided with Napoleon due to prior relations with their former masters. The French exploited these racial disparities to prevent unity among the rebels.

Alexandre Pétion transitioned from serving in the French Colonial Army to becoming a key figure in the fight against French rule. Alongside Toussaint Louverture, Jean-Jacques Dessalines, and Henri Christophe, he rose as an influential military leader who helped establish Haiti's independence. As tensions escalated between Black and mixed-race groups, Toussaint harnessed his authority to gradually seize control of the entire island of Hispaniola. 1803 Napoleon planned to acknowledge Haiti's independence and arranged a meeting with Toussaint Louverture. However, upon his arrival, Toussaint was arrested by Jean-Baptiste Brunet and sent to France.

Napoleon commanded that he be imprisoned in a dungeon in the Jura Mountains, and left to die from starvation. Following Louverture's arrest, African generals and army chiefs decided they would rather die than live under French rule.

After gaining several victories, white plantation owners in Hispaniola started limiting the rights of Blacks and mixed-race individuals. In retaliation, Napoleon committed terrible acts against the formerly enslaved people, including boiling them in molasses, burying them alive, hanging them upside down, drowning them in sacks, and burning captured Haitian soldiers.

In a shocking move, Napoleon invited prominent women to a midnight ball and announced their husbands' horrific deaths. The outcome was disastrous, leading to further humiliation. These degrading acts united formerly enslaved people, mixed-race mulatoos, and Indigenous tribes. Remarkably, some white Polish people joined forces with Jean-Jacques Dessalines—an African-born warrior who succeeded Toussaint Louverture as the rebellion leader—and fought alongside him. By November 1803, the French Army withdrew its remaining troops. Defeated and demoralized colonists fled ahead of the French Army's retreat, while the Haitian rebellion ultimately contributed to Napoleon's army losing its battle against Great Britain.

The invaluable loss led to the Louisiana Purchase, a significant expansion of US territory by acquiring French lands in North America. Those white settlers who didn't support Haiti's liberation were either killed by the Haitian military or exiled to avoid future enslavement. Thanks to Dessalines, Haitian soldiers received some of the white settlers' wealth as war compensation. The assassination of Dessalines, supposedly by Alexandre Pétion and Christophe in 1806, sparked a civil war on Hispaniola. Pétion rallied the mulatto forces in the south, while Henri Christophe led the Black forces in the north.

By 1809, two separate nations emerged on the island. Pétion governed Saint Domingo until he died in 1818, while the eastern part of Hispaniola returned to Spanish control, leaving only the western region under Black African governance. This new nation adopted the indigenous Arawakan name Haiti, meaning "Land of Mountains."

Even though Haiti had freed itself from tyranny and the United States had recently gained independence from Britain, the US allied with France, Spain, and Great Britain to deny Haiti's independence. Despite being a wealthy slave colony previously, this alliance imposed a devastating embargo on Haiti, impeding arms and goods trade. Paying high compensations to European powers and enduring long-term restrictions led to Haiti's unfortunate status as one of the poorest countries in the Western Hemisphere.

> [7] *And when he had opened the fourth seal,*
> *I heard the voice of the fourth beast say, Come and see.*
> [8] *And I looked, and behold a pale horse: and his name that sat on him*
> *was Death, and Hell followed with him. And power was given unto*
> *them over the fourth part of the earth, to kill with sword, and with*
> *hunger, and with death, and with the beasts of the earth.*
>
> *(King James Version, Revelation 6:7-8)*

The wealth of the Americas and Africa played a crucial role in the power shift towards the European economic system. It's hard to imagine that the Europeans' deceitful and self-serving actions could be praised in the name of Christ unless it was for personal gain. Europeans demonstrated their ability to exploit human lives and maintain power through natural selection, leaving their captives helpless. It was truly evil how they managed to control global resources and establish a caste system based on racial dominance.

In his book, *The Origin of Species*, Charles Darwin wrote about how essential structure modifications arise when they benefit an individual in their struggle to survive. This concept parallels Satan's fall from Paradise, as mentioned in the Bible's book of Isaiah and the Quran's AL-Hijr. Suppose people believe that the most powerful being has control over life and death. In that case, they'll go to extreme lengths to become superior and exert power over others, effectively becoming god-like.

Before the Europeans arrived, Africa and the Americas had highly sophisticated cultures and thriving trade networks. They believed that ultimate power belonged to the Sovereign God of the universe. The long-term plan to conquer Africa and the Americas amongst European powers was far from heroic. Recognizing and addressing the deep-rooted hatred that has caused chaos without any sense of justice is cruel. The caste system, a veil for pure malevolence, aimed to elevate the white race while demoting all others to inferior castes. This reprehensible system triggered violence through religious and ethnic clashes, war, and an insatiable hunger for power, ultimately turning death into a common aspect of everyday life.

Most enslaved Africans reached America via the Middle Passage or triangular trade route, enduring devastatingly long trips between six to ten weeks. They were crammed together in atrocious conditions, which led to widespread barbarity, merciless beatings, and rampant disease. Throughout these voyages, enslaved people were confined in unventilated spaces below deck with little regard for cleanliness or basic human dignity. Many refused to eat and were brutally abused by sailors who would use iron devices to force-feed them. Women witnessed their children being discarded overboard as a form of chastisement for insubordination.

During the journey, numerous enslaved people attempted to escape by jumping overboard and swimming ashore, only to be met with heinous cuts, burns from hot coals, or incessant whippings for refusing food. Acts of desperation like these became distressingly frequent as extreme discipline became commonplace. Upon reaching the new world and being forced into submission, enslaved people endured branding with their captor's marks using burning irons. Those who had survived the harrowing 3,000-mile passage were no longer capable of free thought. A campaign of psychological control rendered them helpless before plunging them into unending bondage.

Olaudah Equiano, also known as Gustavus Vassa, recalled the terror and brutality he saw onboard the slave ship as a child:

"The white people looked and acted, as I thought, in so savage a manner; for I had never seen such instances of brutal cruelty among any people."

Equiano noticed the slavers called themselves Christians, and he heard the cries of the enslaved people:

O, ye nominal Christians! Might not an African ask you, "Learned you this from your God, who says unto you, do unto all men as you would men should do to you?" Is it not enough that we are torn from our country and friends to toil for our luxury and lust of gain?

During the harrowing journey on slave ships, African women endured continuous sexual assault by white crew members. The scary sounds of the dying echoed through the ship. Slavers wielded violence, humiliation, and even murder to maintain control. Records indicate that such brutality was widespread, particularly towards young enslaved women. The slavers strived to suppress illegitimate children, deeming them enemies regardless of appearance. Mixed-race offspring were attempting to pass as white-faced severe beatings or even death.

After a profound religious conversion, Reverend John Newton turned against slavery and joined the abolitionist movement. He was demoted to the rank of an ordinary sailor for his defiance and received a dozen lashes. He documented his experiences and convictions in his journal.

When the women and girls are taken on board a ship, naked, trembling, terrified, perhaps almost exhausted with cold, fatigue, and hunger, they are often exposed to the wanton rudeness of white savages...perhaps some hard-hearted pleader may suggest that such treatment would indeed be cruel, in Europe; but the African Women are Negroes, Savages, who have no idea of the nicer sensations which obtain among civilized people.

BRITISH RULE TO AMERICAN FREEDOM

In 1518, a Spanish vessel transported the first Africans to the Americas, where they were sold as enslaved people and forced to work in large labor camps. As Native populations tragically dwindled, Europeans began importing more African captives to fill the void. The increasing demand for sugar led to the expansion of plantations, replacing honey as the primary sweetener in Europe. This new sugar crop greatly impacted the European economy, shifting focus away from gold and precious metals. Settlements created huge agricultural plantations to expand demand for commodities like sugarcane, syrup, tobacco, wheat, and cotton. Since sugar cultivation demanded significant labor, more captives were necessary. These plantations also began producing alcoholic beverages, which were then traded for enslaved Africans and manufactured goods such as guns, whiskey, and fabric.

Tragically, enslaved people were dehumanized and portrayed as savage creatures. White supremacists justified this cruelty by claiming divine ordination. They established a hierarchy with themselves at the top, cementing their dominance through rigid caste structures based on ancestry and appearances.

In Hinduism, the gods ostracized the Untouchables, and contact was strictly prohibited. Dark skin was perceived as a danger to the caste system, and a darker complexion became an excuse for corrupting human values in God's name. The caste hierarchy was founded on a massive deception, with toxic lies woven into the core of society, demonizing the oppressed and glorifying the oppressors. This grand deceit continues to seep through the earth's surface, fueling the persistence of human division. The caste system fundamentally opposes goodness and cannot be associated with anything pure or virtuous. Evil fills the void like a vacuum in the absence of divine presence.

In the Gospel of John, Yeshua the Christ proclaims, "I will leave and return to you." He further adds in John 14:30, "I won't speak much with you any longer, as the world's ruler approaches, but he has no power over Me." The ancient Indo-Europeans who conquered India adhered to a polytheistic faith, appeasing their gods through rituals and creating divine effigies. Interestingly, modern America shares similarities with these early Anglo-Aryan societies, as people pay homage to statues commemorating deceased heroes.

Numerous American architectural marvels and monuments take inspiration from Greco-Roman pagan designs. Confederate statues and other such symbols are perceived by many as representing power and an unspoken divine sanction for white supremacy. This notion of idolatry has long been the foundation of white supremacist beliefs. Satan masterfully manipulates hierarchy to sow discord and tension among humanity. He aims to differentiate the wicked from the righteous, who belong to God. This division creates a pecking order that can lead individuals to stray from God's path and swear loyalty to Satan instead.

The prophet Isaiah, gifted with foresight, offered a heartfelt warning to the Hebrew people about the deceptive agenda of the Gentiles. This striking plea is encapsulated in the following passage:

> *³For your hands are defiled with blood,*
> *And your fingers with iniquity;*
> *Your lips have spoken lies;*
> *Your tongue has muttered perversity.*
> *⁴No one calls for justice, nor does any plead for truth.*
> *They trust in empty words and speak lies;*
> *They conceive evil and bring forth iniquity.*
> *⁵They hatch vipers' eggs and weave the spider's web;*
> *He who eats of their eggs dies,*
> *And from that which is crushed a viper breaks out.*
>
> *(New King James Version, Isaiah 59:3-5)*

Upon their arrival in Africa, Europeans were astounded by the thriving and affluent civilizations they encountered. They weaponized a hierarchical form of Christianity against the African people to exert control. Intrigued and delighted, African leaders embraced this pagan rendition of Christianity, much like Adam succumbing to the temptation of the forbidden fruit in the earthly paradise. They adopted a faith that wasn't part of their roots. Moses cautioned the Hebrews about the future consequences long after he was gone. Africa's fertile lands once sustained the world with its remarkable agricultural prowess. Rome relied on Africa for almost six centuries as a primary food source. Many commodities in America and the Western world sprouted from African soil.

As slave ships departed Africa, valuable natural resources and agricultural goods went with them. Europeans introduced self-hatred, conflict, jealousy, and disarray in exchange, perpetuating internal strife among African descendants. Amidst the slave ship, heart-wrenching cries filled the air as they begged for God's forgiveness and expressed remorse for falling into the white man's twisted trap. They were deceived by his cunning ways and deceptive religious beliefs.

The prophets had cautioned them about this day:

> [28] *"For thus says the Lord God: 'Surely I will deliver you into the hand of those you hate, into the hand of those from whom you alienated yourself.*
> [29] *They will deal hatefully with you, take away all you have worked for, and leave you naked and bare. The nakedness of your harlotry shall be uncovered,*
> *both your lewdness and your harlotry.*
> [30] *I will do these things to you because you have gone as a harlot after the Gentiles, because you have become defiled by their idols.*
>
> *(New King James Version, Ezekiel 23:16-30)*

Ezekiel cautioned the Hebrew women, who admired the Aryans from the Balkans that had arrived in Babylon, that these men would one day return with contempt and cast them into pits. Instead of fleeing from God's wrath, Jeremiah urged the Hebrews to repent for their sins. The white settlers who tossed enslaved people overboard during conflicts on slave ships were descendants of the Aryans from the Balkans.

> [24] *The Lord will change the rain of your land to powder and dust; from the heaven it shall come down on you until you are destroyed.*
> [25] *The Lord will cause you to be defeated before your enemies; you shall go out one way against them and flee seven ways before them; and you shall become troublesome to all the kingdoms of the earth.*
>
> *(New King James Version, Deuteronomy 28: 24-25)*

And;

27 Then the LORD's anger burned against that land,
and he brought against it every curse written in this scroll.
28 The LORD ripped them off their land in anger, wrath, and great fury.
He threw them into other lands, and that's how things still stand today.
(Common English Bible, Deuteronomy 29:27-28)

In the 1600s, the Dutch voyaged to Africa, creating a supply station in present-day Cape Town along their journey to Europe and southern Asia. They expanded their settlements on Africa's southern coast in 1652, taking over land and resources from the local people. The Indigenous Africans faced oppression as the Dutch rose to power in Africa and the Americas for 50 years. South Africa was under Dutch rule until the British seized control in 1795. The Dutch surpassed Portugal in wealth and political stability, becoming Europe's wealthiest merchants. Their initial involvement in the slave trade stemmed from their lust for gold, but soon they rivaled Portugal and France for control over the African Coast.

The Dutch took over many Portuguese forts along Africa's coast, including Elmina Castle, Ghana's first European fort. With the expansion of plantations, Europeans required more enslaved people to manage vast cultivated lands. Native Africans were forced to work on these newly-established plantations. As their primary focus shifted to slave exportation, the Dutch successfully captured plantations in Brazil and dominated the spice trade in Africa. Their thriving shipbuilding industry grew into the world's largest, handling half of Europe's maritime commerce. Immense quantities of gold and silver were mined from Africa and the Americas, ultimately enriching the European economy.

In 1609, the Dutch founded New Netherlands along the Hudson River and established towns across present-day New York, New Jersey, Delaware, and Staten Island. A decade later, in 1619, a Dutch vessel delivered the first enslaved Africans to Jamestown, Virginia, marking their arrival in a British colony. In 1624, Manhattan witnessed the establishment of a Dutch West India Company colony, putting them in competition with France and England. Europeans considered African captives an ideal solution to address their labor shortages and desire for massive wealth.

The Dutch East India Company set up a lasting settlement and supply station at South Africa's Cape of Good Hope (Spice Islands) in 1652. This station facilitated the transportation of goods between Africa and the Americas. Consequently, many Africans relocated from coastal regions to the continent's interior. As the Dutch sought to eliminate the San (Bushmen) and Khoikhoi people from their land, they seized farms and turned captives into enslaved people. While the Bushmen were small-group hunters, the Khoikhoi were farmers and cattle herders. The Europeans almost wiped out, the remaining African tribes as all who wasn't killed abandoned their farms to prevent conflict.

As they expanded further into southern Africa, the Dutch frequently clashed with Zulu tribes. The native people were subjected to armed invasions, seeing their women and children taken captive while European forces destroyed their villages. In 1806, the British took control of the Cape colony, displacing local tribes. However, Shaka, the Zulu king, united surrounding tribes to form a formidable army. A decade later, the Zulus clashed with the British and brokered a temporary peace. At the Battle of Isandhiwana, King Cetshwayo led 20,000 Zulu warriors to victory over the British forces, claiming 2,000 lives.

The British later retaliated with a more powerful army, pushing the Zulus out of their homeland.

Fast forward to 1866, when the largest diamond reserve in the world was discovered in present-day Kimberly, South Africa. Located near the Orange River and aptly named "Big Hole," this mine produced three tons of diamonds. De Beers and Kimberley mines emerged as the world's leading mining companies from this find. Two decades later, in 1886, South Africa struck gold – quite literally – with significant gold deposits in Gauteng Province (Witwatersrand). This discovery led to Johannesburg's establishment and fueled tensions between Dutch settlers and British colonialists competing for precious resources. Britain emerged victorious, seizing resource-rich territories like South Africa's Gold Coast and Ghana from Dutch control. Peter L. Bernstein, in *The Power of Gold*, describes the mining techniques: *"To extract South Africa's annual output of around five hundred tons of gold, some seventy million tons of earth must be raised and milled-an amount greater than all the material in the pyramid of Cheops."*

In a bold quest to conquer present-day Johannesburg, Transvaal, the Orange Free State, and Natal, the British embarked on a thrilling military expedition. As they acquired new territories brimming with riches, a massive labor force was required for mining. Thus, hordes of white foreigners flocked to seize a share of Africa's abundant wealth. Although the slave trade was banned by Britain in 1807, they managed to establish their dominance over the most prominent region on the African continent. The captivating Berlin Conference, convened by German Chancellor Bismarck, aimed to resolve disputes regarding African colonization among European nations. All opposing nations were asked to attend in this historic assembly in order to preserve good relations and avoid bloodshed over Africa's vast continent.

By 1914, the vast African continent had been wholly colonized by European powers, except for Ethiopia and Liberia. Seven major European players - Great Britain, France, Italy, Germany, Belgium, Portugal, and Spain - wrestled for control over various African regions. South Africa witnessed continuous strife between the British and Dutch throughout the tumultuous twentieth century. Meanwhile, Belgium gained exclusive control over the Central African Republic of Congo - leading to a tragic loss of sovereignty for its indigenous people.

White explorers ventured into Africa, discovering abundant resources like diamonds, gold, copper, rubber, ivory, timber, and farms that had been deserted due to the fear of massacre. They also found settlers' establishments such as schools, hospitals, parks, beaches exclusive for whites, and infrastructure that profited from Africa's vast riches.

A similar narrative unfolded throughout the continent. Merciless settlers wrought havoc on women and children alike without exception. The heartbreaking cries of innocent children did nothing to deter their brutality. When Africans rose in opposition, they faced ruthless suppression by the new white governing forces. As Africa's resources were pillaged, many Black Africans were enslaved to serve the Europeans. Forced to labor under grueling conditions, they mined gold, diamonds, copper, and other commodities for the benefit of white settlers. Among the seven major European powers, the British Empire inherited the legacy of the Roman Empire and the African continent.

> [9] *"This calls for wisdom and understanding. The seven heads are seven hills, on which the woman sits. They are also seven kings:*
> [10] *five of them have fallen, one still rules, and the other one has not yet come; when he comes, he must rule only a little while.*
>
> *(Good News Translation, Revelation 17:9-10)*

In 1884, Ethiopia experienced a significant shift from its white, Christian-centered, racially divided power hierarchy. Nehemiah Tile led the Ethiopian Movement, which founded two independent African churches—the Tembu National Church in South Africa and the Independent Ethiopian Church of South Africa—to challenge white supremacy.

This new movement connected Christianity to political activism and introduced an ancient form of Christianity without a caste system. These new religious groups provided Africans with dignity, pride, and opportunities for education, promoting Black unity worldwide.

However, in 1885, Italy invaded Eritrea and established a colony at Massaua (Massawa), trying to control Ethiopia's inland area between the Red Sea and the Nile. As a result, most of Ethiopia's coastal regions were occupied by European settlers. In 1895, the Italian Army attempted to seize the mountain fortress of Amba Alajie but was defeated and forced to retreat. In 1896, Italy sent a massive army of around 20,000 soldiers into northern Ethiopia with the support of the Conference of Berlin.

In reaction to the threat, Ethiopian forces led by Emperor Menelik II gathered 100,000 soldiers to face the Italian Army at the epic Battle of Adwa. They wiped out about 2,000 Italian troops and won. But Ethiopia wasn't out of the woods yet – they had to tackle another crafty European scheme targeting their economy by going after their trade allies. Despite it all, Ethiopia is the only African nation that successfully defended its independence from European invaders during colonization.

¹¹ And the beast that was, and is not,
is himself also the eighth,
and is of the seven,
and is going to perdition.

(New King James Version, Revelation 17: 11*).*

In the 18th century, after Britain triumphed in a seven-year conflict with the French, the 13 British colonies in North America were consumed by an enthusiasm for liberty. United in their resistance to what they viewed as oppressive British rule, these colonies ultimately formed the United States of America. The American Revolution signified a political revolt against Britain's escalating military presence and controversial tax policies. This resistance catalyzed a transformation of thought and liberation from imperial control. Both white and Black communities rallied against the British government, aiming to dismantle the inequalities and limitations imposed by slave codes. Together, the colonies fought against the British Crown.

Valuing local representation and equitable commerce, the colonists aimed to break free from Britain's restrictive trade practices. They wished to compete and broaden their market, while Britain limited them to trade exclusively with England. With many enslaved people skilled in growing rice, tobacco, cotton, and other agricultural goods, the colonists gained an edge in their pursuit of independence. As Britain upheld the gold standard for legal tender, the colonies introduced paper bills – a move promptly quashed by Britain.

CHAPTER NINE

The Abolitionist Movement: Battling Slavery and Racial Inequality

Tensions between British soldiers and American colonists erupted in Boston in 1770. During a protest outside the Custom House, formerly enslaved person and dock worker Crispus Attucks stood up against the soldiers. The crowd started with snowballs, but things quickly escalated. Eventually, a soldier fired a shot, and Attucks and four other men died in what came to be known as the tragic Boston Massacre. Seven years earlier, the British had imposed unpopular taxes on the colonists to pay off defense debts from the Seven Years' War. This included the Stamp Act of 1765, which required tax stamps on all legal and commercial documents. Colonists were outraged and refused to pay, leading to the famous cry of "No taxation without representation."

In April 1775, the American Revolutionary War began when the colonists took control of the government and expelled the

British officials from Lexington and Concord, Massachusetts. Imagine a stirring tapestry of courage and unity woven by a diverse tapestry of individuals hailing from various townships, bound together by an unwavering resolve to fight for freedom and defy oppression. These valiant souls, known as the Patriots, embodied the vibrant mosaic of races that comprised their ranks. Their collective spirit resonated across the American colonies, inspiring all who yearned for liberation. From every corner of the colonies, they joined forces, forged alliances, and braved the unrestrained tempest of rebellion. Their shared vision of a brighter future fueled their fight against tyranny and kindled the flames of liberty that continue to burn bright in the chronicles of history.

However, the path to independence was not without its complexities. Surprisingly, nearly half of the American colonists, known as the Tories, remained loyal to the British Empire. These loyalists, standing shoulder to shoulder with British troops, presented a formidable challenge to the Patriots' quest for emancipation.

The loyalists, often educated and wealthy elites, believed that independence from the British would mean the loss of economic prosperity and feared that America's colonies would become ungovernable or tyrannical. In contrast, the Patriots saw the loyalists as traitors. Enraged colonists often attacked the loyalists due to their support for the British and suffered greatly.

During the Revolutionary War, most Native Americans fought with the British against the colonies because of their trade alliances, with the Iroquois tribe being the largest of the groups. The Natives believed a victorious British government would be more likely to honor their trade agreements and policies than the colonies, which tended to break treaties and encroach on Native land. However, despite their contributions to the British forces, the Natives had little to no influence on the post-war policies set forth by the British government. This lack of recognition and appreciation led to further tension between the Natives and the new American government.

In the early battles of Lexington, Concord, Fort Ticonderoga, and Bunker Hill, enslaved African Americans courageously fought and triumphed alongside white soldiers. However, the tides soon changed, with the colonists facing crushing losses in New York, New Jersey, and Pennsylvania. To make matters worse, enslaved individuals who were captured fighting in the war faced brutal consequences, either being sent back to their owners or killed in retribution for joining the British side. Despite these challenges, black soldiers displayed exceptional bravery and prowess on the battlefield. Their tales of heroism eventually convinced Rhode Island to defy Washington and permit enslaved people to join their ranks.

By 1777, after a series of British victories, Washington finally acknowledged the importance of Black soldiers for the American colonies. As a result, he enacted laws that allowed enslaved individuals to earn their freedom by serving in the Continental Army, granting them a chance to fight for their own liberty as the colonies' future hung in the balance.

On July 2, 1776, the thirteen colonies united in Philadelphia to decide their fate – should they break free from Britain's grip? The United States Declaration of Independence was born on July 4, 1776, transforming the former British colonies into a sovereign nation. Spain and France didn't hesitate to lend a hand once independence was declared. In fact, the French government went the extra mile, signing three treaties to help the colonists stand on their own two feet. The Netherlands soon joined the fray against Britain too. However, in a twist of events on May 12, 1780, 5,000 American troops found themselves surrendering in Charleston, South Carolina.

The Battle of Bunker Hill turned out to be one of the war's most brutal clashes. The British faced a staggering loss as they struggled to claim the hill near Boston. About 1,100 British soldiers fell during the fierce combat; even though they managed to seize Bunker Hill after several attempts, it marked a major turning point in the conflict.

In a decisive moment, the British Army fell in Yorktown, Virginia, on October 19, 1781. This defeat made Britain realize their efforts were futile. Finally, on April 19, 1783, the Continental Congress sealed a peace treaty with Great Britain. Paralleling the rise of the Roman Empire, the United States emerged as the sole nation fitting all characteristics of the enigmatic biblical Babylon. Rising from 13 British colonies, it became a powerful force shaping global legal systems and championing freedom – vital pillars of our civilization. Like with any nation, abiding by common laws is essential for a society's survival and success.

During the Revolutionary War, people of all races came together, fighting for liberty and equality against the British who oppressed the colonists. The Declaration of Independence pledged the rights to life, liberty, and the pursuit of happiness. Yet, many enslaved individuals battled and perished for their own freedom which they were promised but ultimately denied. After the war, numerous escaped slaves were returned to their owners, while others have come to feel that the caste system had little to do with European dominance. Even so, some still think that the perceived inferiority of Black individuals is responsible for their lower socio-economic status.

Throughout history, the incredible achievements and cultural impact of Black individuals in America have often been disregarded or diminished. Our nation's early days were marred by unfulfilled promises of freedom for Black people, which could have alleviated past wrongs if carried out. The intricate societies of both Europe and America depended on the involvement of Africans and Native peoples, irrespective of their desire to take part.

Unfortunately, some people fail to see that racism and inequality were the driving forces behind the fall of Rome. Racism is a destructive toxin, leading to heinous acts, deception, and suppression. While we have come far since the founding of America, issues like Paganism and systemic racism remain deeply ingrained within our nation's core

While Rome symbolizes a significant aspect of America's history, it's impossible to overlook the negative impacts of prejudice and elitism. During the first century BC., everyday citizens took to Rome's streets to challenge the class system and advocate for governmental reforms, giving rise to civil wars. Our modern government structures are deeply rooted in Roman practices, even incorporating slave labor in their construction. The United States today is characterized by a glaring wealth disparity between white and Black citizens – with the average white family earning ten times more than a Black family, irrespective of their education levels. This systemic racism and entrenched white privilege have not only robbed many Black individuals of their freedom but have also made it difficult for them to achieve financial stability.

Nowadays, the spotlight is on protests against racial injustice, emphasizing the deep-rooted racism and militarization in Black communities, even after 160 years since emancipation. Historically, segregation led to African Americans experiencing limited job security, inadequate healthcare, homeownership barriers, and restricted access to financial resources for a better life. For some, progress in liberty for Black individuals and other minorities has been stagnant for far too long. The notion of a caste system remains deeply ingrained in the minds of many white people in America. Interestingly, the American caste system shares numerous similarities with India's Hindu caste system. The United States was established around 3,500 years after the Aryans came out of the Balkans during the end of the Ice Age.

The epic journey of migration ultimately culminated in the conquest of the land we now know as India, dedicated to Indra, the mighty god of war. Tracing their lineage and language back to the Aryans, and those intrepid white settlers who embarked on voyages across the Atlantic Ocean to reached the shores of North and South America. As these ancient explorers settled in the Indus Valley, the caste system's complex social hierarchy emerged, giving birth to a framework of subjugation. This structure favored the white power base, elevating them to the summit of societal rankings while confining Black and brown individuals to the base of this human stratification pyramid. Propelled by divine guidance or merely driven by self-deception, the white Anglo-Saxons assumed an authoritative role in this dominant caste as they claimed their perceived supremacy.

When the pilgrims settled in Plymouth, Massachusetts, the Native Americans helped them adapt to their new home by teaching essential skills like farming, fishing, and hunting. Together, they celebrated a bountiful harvest, marking the first Thanksgiving and a peace pact between them. As time passed, the settlers' population and farmlands expanded due to profitable crops like corn, wheat, and tobacco.

This expansion led to land grabbing and tensions that sparked armed conflicts with the Native Americans. As settlers formed alliances and continued expanding their territory, life for the Native Americans became more challenging, with many being captured and labeled prey. Following the Revolutionary War, Native Americans living in regions such as western Mississippi, western Carolinas, northern Georgia, eastern Alabama, Tennessee, and Florida were forcibly uprooted by the US government. They were then relocated to reservations in Arkansas and Oklahoma. However, many Cherokees, Choctaws, and Seminoles resisted relocation, choosing instead to join other Indigenous tribes and engage in battles along Florida's coastline.

Eventually, seeking shelter in the Everglades, these groups remained in their Florida homeland. The Seminole Wars, which started in 1816 under the command of Andrew Jackson, Florida's first governor, were prompted by their resistance and unwillingness to return fugitive enslaved people. These conflicts ultimately took a heavy toll on the US government's finances and the lives of numerous soldiers. After the Revolutionary War, Native Americans occupying the west of Mississippi, the western Carolinas, northern Georgia, eastern Alabama, Tennessee, and Florida were removed by force from their homes and relocated by the U.S. government.

Many Cherokees, Choctaw, and Seminoles opposed relocation and joined forces with other Indigenous tribes. They fiercely battled along Florida's coast, eventually finding sanctuary in the Everglades and staying in their cherished homeland. Their resistance, which included refusing to hand over fugitive enslaved people, created the groundwork for the brutal Seminole Wars. These wars began in 1816 under Andrew Jackson's rule as the first governor of Florida and drained the United States' resources and lives. In a surprising twist, several Seminole natives surrendered to the U.S. Army once America bought Florida from Spain. These Indigenous tribes were forcibly relocated to Arkansas and Oklahoma. When gold was discovered in Minnesota, many Sioux and Cheyenne Indians faced a similar fate, as they too were moved to Oklahoma by the U.S. government to reservations in Arkansas and Oklahoma.

In an attempt to negotiate a peace treaty and gain U.S. military protection, Chief Black Kettle and Chief Antelope of the Cheyenne tribe met with the governor regarding the Sand Creek conflict. They were instructed to return to their camp, where soldiers would ensure their safety. Both chiefs signed the Fort Wise Treaty in September 1860 to resolve increasing tensions between Indigenous Americans and white settlers before the Civil War. These tensions were fueled by settlers encroaching on native lands, leading to a food shortage for Native populations.

However, on November 29, 1864, Colorado Governor John Evans commanded Colonel John Chivington, a former Denver minister, to forcefully remove the Natives from their territory. Under cover of the night, soldiers surrounded the Native camp and shot those attempting to flee. Chivington instructed his troops to show no mercy; soldiers tortured and killed almost every Native present in what would become known as the Third Colorado Cavalry massacre.

The scene was horrifying, as the Indigenous people fell victim to brutal sword attacks, with limbs and heads severed mercilessly. Soldiers proudly displayed the scalps of their victims, primarily women and children, who comprised two-thirds of those killed. Colonel Chivington cold-heartedly dragged the defenseless bodies through blood-soaked streets. In the end, Chief Antelope experienced unimaginable torment at the hands of the soldiers, driven by their immense hatred. They maimed his body, cutting off his nose, ears, and testicles.

THE STRUGGLE FOR EDUCATION AND LIBERATION

Throughout the American Abolitionist Movement, abolitionists took a strong stand against discrimination. They launched a widespread crusade to battle the horrors of slavery, oppression, and racial inequality. In most Southern states, enslaved people were deliberately kept uneducated; those found learning to read faced brutal consequences, such as severe beatings or even limb amputations. Nonetheless, learning to read and write gave enslaved people a vital weapon for successful communication and, eventually, the desire for liberation. Established in 1817, the American Colonization Society sought to end slavery by encouraging or forcing the relocation of enslaved individuals to Liberia or Sierra Leone in Africa. In support of this objective, the group encouraged Congress to deport Black people to Africa, the Caribbean, or any other acceptable site selected by legislators.

The movement struggled to find support among abolitionists, primarily due to the prevailing belief that Blacks were inferior and should live separately from whites. Although the British had successfully founded Sierra Leone in 1787 as a haven for repatriated Blacks, the American Colonization Society failed to win the trust of the Abolitionist Movement. By 1807, the United Kingdom abolished slavery, prompting thousands of enslaved Africans to flee to the Bahamas, southeast of Florida, where they established an agriculture-based economy. Regrettably, not all abolitionists were on board with the Return to Africa Movement, and many native-born Black Americans viewed the United States as their true home. Repatriating freed enslaved people to Africa could have offered an escape from racism and alleviated white fears of liberated Blacks in America.

Paul Cuffee, a passionate advocate and activist, fervently supported sending freed African Americans back to Africa. He aimed to overcome racial issues by forging trade connections between Britain and America. For enslavers, this movement promised to quell possible uprisings and alleviate concerns about escaped or freed enslaved people. Born of Indigenous American and African heritage, Cuffee was a prosperous ship-owner who personally funded an expedition to West Africa. Although he passed away in 1817, his dream lived on, as Liberia eventually gained independence in 1847. His relentless efforts enabled the relocation of 11,000 formerly enslaved people to West Africa.

Abolitionists were determined to exploit every possible avenue to eradicate the scourge of slavery. As their crusade progressed, many enslaved individuals grew increasingly rebellious, fueling more radical movements that sought to end slavery. The hatred within Black America towards systemic oppression intensified, and people became unafraid to risk everything for their freedom. In 1739, America witnessed its first major rebellion in South Carolina on a British colony. Led by Jemmy, an African-born slave, a team of freedom fighters assembled near the Stono River. They raided a store for weapons and ammunition before starting their mission, chanting "Liberty." As they journeyed from one plantation to another, they eliminated overseers, and liberated fellow enslaved people. The revolt left roughly 25 whites and 35 enslaved Africans dead. Such insurrections inspired caution among slaveholders and led them to punish the rebels involved hastily.

One of the most remarkable uprisings in American history was led by Nat Turner, a self-taught preacher and enslaved person who believed he had received divine guidance to free his people from enslavement. Turner devised a clever strategy that involved other enslaved people joining forces to establish an independent Black army. However, white mobs perceived these rebellions as defying God's will and deserving punishment by divine power. According to the beliefs of these white people, they were entitled to seize possessions from Black and brown individuals and maintain their economic suppression, all in the name of religion.

The Nat Turner Revolts killed around 60 white slaveholders and their family members but excluded poor whites. Despite only lasting a few days, Turner evaded capture until October 30, 1831.

As the abolitionist movement gained momentum, activists harnessed the power of newspapers, poetry, and personal narratives to expose the savage realities of slavery. This allowed enslaved individuals to share their experiences in their own words. People of all races, united by their moral convictions, rallied behind the anti-slavery cause and even offered safe refuge for escapees.

William Lloyd Garrison, a staunch Christian, founded his newspaper titled "The Liberator," where he condemned slavery by referencing the Book of Isaiah, labeling it as "a covenant with death," and denouncing America's Constitution. Tragically, in 1837, Presbyterian minister Elijah Parrish Lovejoy paid the ultimate price for his work when a white mob attempted to confiscate his printing press after publishing an article about a lynching in St. Louis. Despite being shot five times and severely injured, Lovejoy valiantly defended his warehouse before succumbing to his injuries in Alton, Illinois. His sacrifice speaks volumes about the courageous men and women who were part of the American Anti-Slavery Society.

Many artistic works thrived, with men and women, both Black and white, participating in a changing role to condemn the brutality and ignorance of slavery. Many abolitionists' homes became shelters for the Underground Railroad to help escaped enslaved people fleeing to the Free States or Canada. In 1804, Haiti (previously known as Saint-Domingue) proudly proclaimed its independence, ending French control and the appalling practice of slavery. As the first sovereign Latin American nation and the Western Hemisphere's second democracy, Haiti's inspiring move to abolish slavery had a tremendous global impact, particularly in the United States.

Northern states quickly took action, ending slavery outright or implementing plans to become slave-free territories. This incredible wave of liberation transformed the future of slavery and the pursuit of freedom worldwide. In 1807, the United Kingdom followed suit, banning the Atlantic slave trade and actively intercepting slave ships departing from Africa. The Civil War tore the nation apart, fueled by clashing beliefs and leading to rifts within families. It also created a divide in the Abolitionist Movement between radical and idealistic abolitionists.

The war pitted the Southern States, known as the Confederate States of America, who fought for their right to maintain an economy based on agriculture, against the Northerners who sought a modern, industrialized lifestyle. As Great Britain and France abolished slavery, moral opposition grew in the North. Abolitionists saw this period as their chance to eradicate the cruel oppression of slavery. Among the most revered radical abolitionists was John Brown, who launched a daring raid on a federal armory in Harper's Ferry, Virginia, in 1859. He hoped to spark slave uprisings and put an end to slavery. Believing it was his Christian duty, Brown was committed to abolishing slavery at all costs. His father, Owen Brown, advocated for the Underground Railroad and raised his son to view slavery as a wicked institution that would one day face divine retribution.

Before his assault on the federal armory, John Brown sought retribution for a previous attack that demolished the printing presses of two pro-freedom newspapers and set ablaze an abolitionist's hotel in Lawrence, Kansas. Established by anti-slavery advocates from Massachusetts in 1854, Lawrence became a hotbed of violence as proslavery settlers despised newly-freed enslaved people's rights in the territory, and Sheriff Samuel J. Jones led them. John Brown targeted William Doyle's home, capturing him and his son, who were later discovered brutally murdered nearby. Brown and his followers embarked on a four-year quest against slavery; they vowed to keep fighting till their dying breaths in any slave-owning state.

Upon arriving at Harper's Ferry, Brown's group swiftly overran the armory, distributing weapons to enslaved people for an ill-fated rebellion known as the Pottawatomie Massacre. Contrary to Brown's expectations, not many enslaved people joined his uprising. He was convinced that it was his divine duty to eradicate slavery. During their revolt, Brown and his cohorts killed five men, liberated 30 enslaved people, and took Colonel L.W. Washington—George Washington's great-grandnephew—hostage. The formerly enslaved people were coerced into taking up arms, resulting in one of them drowning while attempting to escape. Pro-slavery mobs from nearby towns arrived to back residents; consequently, Brown and his gang took refuge in a neighboring firehouse amid heavy gunfire.

President Buchanan deployed Robert E. Lee and some marines to suppress the chaos. Tragically, two of Brown's sons perished in the battle, while another had died earlier defending formerly enslaved people near Osawatomie against white slaveholders from Missouri. John Brown, convicted of treason, faced the gallows as a traitor. Throughout his trial, his unwavering religious devotion and a fiery speech against slavery's atrocities captured public attention, kindling compassion for abolitionists in the North. Moments before his execution, John Brown uttered these poignant words:

> *Now, if it is deemed necessary that I should forfeit my life for the furtherance of the ends of justice and MINGLE MY BLOOD FURTHER WITH THE BLOOD OF MY CHILDREN, and with the blood of millions in this Slave country, whose rights are disregarded by wicked, cruel, and unjust enactments, —I say LET IT BE DONE.*

During Fredrick Douglass's 1882 speech in Harper's Ferry, Virginia, he credited John Brown for beginning the American Civil War that finally ended slavery and called him one of America's greatest heroes.

The Great Frederick Douglass paid homage to Mr. John Brown, saying,

> *His zeal in the cause of freedom was infinitely superior to mine. Mine was a tapered light; his was the burning sun. Mine was bounded by time, his stretched away to the silent shores of eternity. I could speak for the slave. John Brown could fight for the slave. I could live for the slave. John Brown could die for the enslaved person.*
>
> *(Blight, n.d.)*

The Road to Emancipation and the Abolition of Slavery

In November 1860, Lincoln became president with just 40% of the popular vote but secured 59% of the electoral vote, receiving no support from Southern states. The South saw Lincoln as a secret abolitionist, and soon after his victory, they discussed seceding from the Union. While Lincoln thought the Constitution barred the federal government from meddling in states where slavery was present, he also believed new states shouldn't have the right to permit slavery. Like many Northerners, Lincoln opposed extending slavery to the North, yet he wouldn't demand abolishing it where it was already established.

The South didn't want their rights and state powers questioned by the federal government. The South felt unrepresented at the federal level and compelled to handle their security and economic affairs independently. Under Abraham Lincoln's leadership, the Republican Party opposed slavery's expansion and denounced the disunion threat. Lincoln understood that Americans had various disagreements beyond just slavery, and the country had turned into a divided household. During his campaign, he argued that the nation should either forsake slavery entirely or accept it. Lincoln emphasized that if the Union led to war, the primary goal would be preserving the Union, not eliminating slavery. He officially took office in March 1861.

By April 12, 1861, Confederate forces attacked Fort Sumter in Charleston Harbor, South Carolina. The Confederates hoped Great Britain and France would support them against the Union as both nations relied on the South's textile business. Charles Francis Adams, John Quincy Adams' son, persuaded Britain not to acknowledge the Confederacy as an independent nation and to steer clear of the conflict. Lincoln sent captured enslaved people back to the South in the war's early stages. Abolitionists criticized him for prioritizing Union preservation over slavery issues and pressured President Lincoln to admit that slavery was the primary cause of the American Civil War.

Numerous German immigrants, having faced persecution, showed empathy towards enslaved people, which led to their involvement in the Abolitionist Movement during the Civil

War. Their expertise in machinery granted the Union a strategic advantage when Lincoln integrated railroads, telegraphs, and steamships into the war efforts. Confederate martial law and strict draft in Texas sparked a rebellion among German immigrants. Many fled north to support the Union or escaped south to Mexico. A group heading to Mexico experienced a brutal attack near Fort Clark by Confederate soldiers in an event now called the Nueces Massacre.

The war raged on, with massive casualties at the Battle of Antietam. Lincoln eventually issued an ultimatum: he would free all enslaved people in Confederate territories unless the South rejoined the Union by January 1, 1863. This tactic aimed to weaken the Southern economy and force their hand; however, it remained a violent act against Blacks. On September 22, 1862, President Lincoln made a historic decision by signing the Emancipation Proclamation. This impactful document declared freedom for all enslaved people in seceded territories from January 1, 1863. However, enslaved people in Union territories remained enslaved. Tensions were high, as the new ruling was a compromise for states battling the North but still wanting to hold onto their 'right' to enslave people. For African Americans, it was clear that nothing less than true independence would suffice.

The brutal conflict between the North and South saw numerous casualties. Desperate to break free from their chains, many enslaved people fled Southern plantations during the chaos. This flight sparked fear of a rebellion among colonists, with plantation owners growing increasingly worried that formerly enslaved people would seek vengeance on those who had once owned them. As the war neared its end, heated debates emerged, and some aimed to cast the struggle for freedom in a more symbolic light. Countless abolitionists and military leaders were crucial in organizing all-Black regiments led by white commanders. These fearless groups greatly affected the outcome for the North as they fought for their cause. Formerly enslaved people possessed invaluable knowledge of Southern territories and used this knowledge to become exceptional scouts for the Union forces.

The tide finally turned against slavery, but the South was relentless, punishing any Blacks seeking refuge in the North and returning escapees to even harsher bondage to deter others from joining the Union. Many runaways served in the Union Army, with around 35,000 Black soldiers sacrificing their lives and 23 honored with the prestigious Medal of Honor. The Civil War, which ranged from 1861 to 1865, became the deadliest conflict in American history, claiming 620,000 soldiers. A pivotal moment arrived on February 1, 1865, when President Lincoln signed the Thirteenth Amendment, eradicating slavery. This landmark legislation was ratified on December 18 of the same year, declaring slavery illegal nationwide. Much like Julius Caesar's fateful crossing of the Rubicon that triggered a civil war in ancient Rome, there was no going back. The course of history had been irreversibly altered.

CHAPTER TEN

The American Civil War: Division, Emancipation, and the Transformation of a Nation

Throughout the Reconstruction period, African-Americans owned land and took part in elected positions. Many formerly enslaved people overcame obstacles to achieve political offices and economic progress. Seventeen of them were successfully elected to the U.S. Congress. In March 1865, to support African Americans and impoverished whites in the South, Congress established the Freedman's Bureau. The organization was responsible for providing healthcare services and education since laws had previously prevented enslaved people from accessing literacy and primary health rights. As a result, schools and hospitals were set up across the region. Before his untimely death, President Lincoln sought to pass legislation dividing confiscated land into 40-acre plots for distribution among formerly enslaved people. Back in 1867, a bold Republican congressman named Thaddeus Stevens came up with an exciting plan. He proposed a bill to break up large Southern plantations worth over $5,000 and distribute them as small farmlands to Black families. This revolutionary idea aimed to genuinely free former slaves and give them a fresh start. Unfortunately, President Lincoln's assassination hindered the progress of these bills.

Countless African-American farmers embraced sharecropping as a means to progress, dividing 50% of their yield with landowners in return for land access. Despite its obstacles and potential to thrust formerly enslaved individuals into poverty, sharecropping enabled these farmers to earn without fixed wages while gaining autonomy from close supervision. The shadow of white privilege loomed, seeking to reassert dominance over Black people by promoting slavery or an apartheid America throughout the nation's core. Nonetheless, abolitionists and Black individuals prioritized immediate liberation and emancipation. Persistent efforts were made to keep control over Black lives by hindering their journey towards freedom and wealth accumulation. Apartheid remained ingrained in America from its inception until its demise.

Determined radicals in Congress fought for Black rights by advocating for their voting rights, believing it would ensure physical and political freedom instead of relying on individual states. During Reconstruction, numerous racial barriers that kept Black people in bondage were confronted in court. 1866 Congress enacted the Civil Rights Act over President Andrew Johnson's veto, expanding the Freedman Bureau's powers. These new laws granted the Freedman Bureau authority to offer educational opportunities and safeguard formerly enslaved people's civil rights in southern states. This crucial victory ensured racial prejudice wouldn't be entwined within written laws. Consequently, the Constitution expanded beyond white exclusivity, and Black emancipation became more than a haunting lyric of terror and darkness.

In the summer of 1866, the 14th Amendment was passed by Congress, ensuring that both federal and state laws treated Blacks and whites equally. A few years later, in 1869, the 15th Amendment was proposed and eventually ratified in 1870, making it illegal to deny citizens the right to vote based on their race. Congress also banned discrimination on public transportation and enacted laws to safeguard formerly enslaved people from labor exploitation.

By 1868, seven southern states – Tennessee, Alabama, Florida, Arkansas, Louisiana, North Carolina, and South Carolina – had fulfilled the necessary conditions to rejoin the Union. The remaining Confederate states followed suit in 1870 after ratifying the 15th Amendment. As many Southerners opposed these amendments and chose not to engage in politics, Black politicians gradually replaced them. The idea of equal rights for Black people was unbearable to many white individuals who couldn't fathom living under such circumstances or even being governed by them. In South Carolina, a notably racist state, the majority-Black population resulted in a legislature dominated by Black politicians. Some white Southerners who had lost their land refused to partake in the rebuilding process after the Civil War.

In 1866, Nathan Bedford Forrest, an ex-Confederate general and former slave trader, led a group of planters and bigoted leaders in forming a clandestine organization called the Ku Klux Klan in Pulaski, Tennessee. Their primary objective was to terrorize, attack, and murder Black individuals and their supporters. The organization, also known as the "Invisible Empire of the South," mainly consisted of Confederate soldiers who aimed to prevent African Americans from leaving the South and establishing equality under the law. Klansmen, in their armed groups, actively targeted Black political figures in a relentless pursuit to maintain white supremacy through terror. These groups resorted to violent means to prevent Black individuals from voting and burned down schools and churches connected to the Freedmen Bureau.

A strong sense of superiority compelled many Southern whites to champion a legal system that discriminated against African Americans – denying them the right to education and certain liberties, effectively keeping them separate from the white population. As the Union Army made its way through the South, Black communities rose to power, igniting a fiery response from radical Republicans thirsty for wartime revenge. However, the Klan vehemently fought against these newfound rights by implementing their dual legal system, effectively placing the law under their control.

Despite the achievements of Black communities during Reconstruction, the Klan utilized lynch mob trials as a chilling warning for them not to breach established social boundaries. The KKK and similar white supremacist groups spread across the United States, infiltrating law enforcement and government agencies to gain political and societal influence, further promoting racial segregation. They frequently targeted innocent individuals, establishing numerous Jim Crow laws aimed at intimidating, degrading, and controlling the Black community.

From 1860 to 1920, over 5,000 lynchings occurred, with some victims being whites who were closely associated with Black individuals. The legislation was enacted to restrict Black people from entering various business professions, obtaining skilled labor positions, or owning property. The initial goal of the Jim Crow system was to undermine any economic advancements or social progress made by African Americans. Black code laws sought to reinstate a form of slavery through a cruel set of regulations that governed every aspect of African American life. Within the Vagrancy Law, all Black individuals between 18 and 60 must provide written proof of employment to avoid being charged with a criminal offense. If unable to pay the resulting fine, they would be "hired out" to any white person willing to cover the fine's cost.

The Black Code laws severely limited the freedom of African Americans, requiring written permission to travel beyond their hometowns and prohibiting their access to public spaces designated for whites only, such as parks, schools, restaurants, and hotels. White people were encouraged to avoid interacting with Black individuals by denying them service or forcing them to use separate entrances.

The rise of racist organizations can largely be attributed to Andrew Johnson, a Democratic Senator from Tennessee who assumed the presidency following Lincoln's death. Johnson contended that Senate Bill No. 60, proposed at the end of the Civil War, never meant for the federal government to provide necessities and education for formerly enslaved people. The rapid progress alarmed white Southerners, who called upon the Black Code to slow things down. The implementation of the Black Code aimed to enforce racial segregation legally and strip away any civil rights African Americans gained during Reconstruction. Consequently, white Southerners regained political power while African Americans were denied citizenship rights.

Under the Black Code, black people saw their property confiscated and were frequently coerced into working for their previous enslavers. Those who resisted found themselves subject to brutal violence in the form of lynching, beatings, or burnings. To intimidate black communities further, Klan members held demonstrations wearing hoods and carrying crosses in predominantly African American neighborhoods. Mobs targeted black homes and violently attacked or killed any African American individual they believed was progressing in society.

In March 1877, Rutherford B. Hayes became president after a controversial election where he lost the popular vote but was awarded the majority of electoral votes. Despite promising to protect the rights of Black people and rebuild the Republican Party in the South, his presidency saw a stark reversal of these vows.

Hayes' administration marked the end of Reconstruction and returned the South to autonomous governance. The Republican Party abandoned its support for Black rights, and Congress denied funding for federal troops and U.S. Marshals needed in the region. With national forces withdrawn, white supremacists regained control, ending the period of post-Civil War rebuilding.

White supremacists seized power at polling stations and used political violence to deter Black voters. Black citizens faced violent attacks during mass protests, often resulting in gruesome imagery involving lynchings. As the Roman Catholic Church distanced itself from racist ideologies, it lost its status as the dominant religion. When African Americans tried to leave the South, they faced outrage from white bigots who threatened violence against those providing transport.

Despite being needed for cheap labor in the South, white people often treated Black workers poorly. Elected officials and law enforcement agents ignored laws promoting equality among races. The U.S. Supreme Court even supported racial segregation and formalized discrimination nationwide.

On March 6, 1857, the Supreme Court denied Dred Scott's effort to secure freedom for himself, his wife, and their daughters under Chief Justice Roger B. Taney. In a case upholding Missouri's ruling, Taney infamously declared that Black individuals were inferior beings with no rights that white people should acknowledge.

After his enslaver's death and the refusal of his owner's widow to provide emancipation documents, Dred Scott had been left with Henry Blow—an abolitionist fighting for Scott's freedom—by Emerson's widow. In rejecting Scott's appeal, the High Court limited the constitutional rights for Black individuals while maintaining privileges for whites, preventing mixed-race marriages, and upholding racial dominance.

In the early 1900s, African Americans leveraged tensions among European nations to demand human rights. As many migrated northwards in search of opportunity, they faced challenges adapting to urban life and industry constraints. Organizations like the National Urban League (formed in 1910) and the NAACP (established in 1909) sought to assist these individuals and combat segregation by promoting education, protests, and voter registration. United by a common cause, white and Black activists worked together to challenge discriminatory laws and foster racial equality.

The Harlem Renaissance was a vibrant merging of politics, economics, music, theatre, literature, visual arts, and African American culture. Primarily centered in Harlem during the 1920s and 1930s, its influence spread nationwide. This movement showcased African Americans' talents and debunked racial stereotypes and myths about Black people.

Thriving Harlem nightlife attracted many white visitors to Manhattan Island, just north of Central Park. They enjoyed the entertainment catering to diverse audiences and celebrated

African American artistry until the early morning. The Harlem Renaissance enabled Black individuals to connect with their true African heritage and take pride in their racial identity.

Numerous groups were formed to resist prejudice and solve social and racial issues confronting African Americans. In the early 1900s, various Black Hebrew groups identified spiritually with the children of Israel. They recognized their historical roots within ancient Hebrew beliefs that all Blacks were part of the Hebrew race.

In the South, marriages between Black and white individuals were deemed illegal and seen as a threat to white lineage. During the Jim Crow era, the one-drop rule forbade interracial relations, stating that anyone with even a drop of Black blood was considered non-white. This led to the belief that a single drop of concealed Black blood could dramatically change people's perception of someone's race. Consequently, the fear of discovering this hidden Black heritage could label even the wealthiest white individuals as Black. These laws aimed to maintain the so-called purity of the Caucasian race. Many chose to remain silent, aware that they were descended from mixed ancestry.

During the Jim Crow era, white supremacists in the South exploited existing hypocrisy to reestablish political and social control after Reconstruction. It was widespread for white men to give in to lustful desires and commit sexual transgressions against enslaved women, fathering biracial children without remorse since the dawn of slavery. Across the nation, African American lives were lost to jealousy, deceit, and racial prejudice. Being Black meant constantly battling against segregation, social injustice, and humiliation. Labelling Blacks as inferior paved the way for cruel acts during these conflicts. Ultimately, Jim Crow laws aimed to subdue African Americans under a caste system, keeping them physically and mentally suppressed.

After World War I, Black soldiers who had fought for human rights abroad returned home to combat racial prejudice in America. The post-war period saw political leaders, Black entrepreneurs, and everyday African Americans rally against bigotry, discrimination, and racially motivated violence. They committed their support to numerous groups fighting against Jim Crow laws. A new generation of determined Black individuals rose to make a stand for their rights and change the course of history.

Stores with predominantly Black clientele refused to employ Black workers and were met with boycotts. Yet, many white individuals couldn't accept the idea of racial integration or compromise for Black people's social and economic advancement. During protests, numerous African Americans in the South confronted Confederate flags, experiencing a sense of freedom as some families became divided over their support for civil rights following the war. Ultimately, the movement led to a considerable shift in awareness across all races, shaping a symbolic representation of authentic America.

Despite the ongoing war, a large number of white individuals held the belief that Black people were inferior and required control. Prestigious vigilante groups, like the Ku Klux Klan, emerged to regulate Black people through fear tactics. Whenever African American progress threatened the existing order, these vigilantes would resort to punishment and intimidation.

Interracial relationships were severely punished, such as imprisonment, public humiliation, or even lynching. The 1920s saw a spike in violence against African Americans, with brutal acts often treated like spectator sports – Black individuals were hunted down and subjected to public whippings. In some cases, they were pulled from their jail cells and either hanged or burned alive by enraged white crowds.

In many Southern states, Klansmen dressed in their hooded uniforms would storm Black-owned businesses and force their owners to sell up and leave town. Legal provisions made it impossible for Black people to testify against whites, allowing law enforcement officers to partake in these heinous acts without repercussions.

Shockingly, local newspapers would sometimes advertise lynchings, drawing white men, women, and children as spectators. The Ku Klux Klan heavily influenced communities in the South, and biased politicians quickly justified these violent actions. It wasn't uncommon for a noose to be used as a tool of fear or for a Black individual to be hanged at the whim of the Klan. This brutal behavior reinforced white superiority and perpetuated racial dominance.

In 1921, Greenwood, also known as Black Wall Street, was situated just across the Frisco railroad tracks from Tulsa, Oklahoma. A furious white mob unleashed a brutal wave of violence upon African Americans. On May 30th, Memorial Day, a young and sharply dressed 19-year-old Black man named Dick Rowland entered the Drexel Building on South Main Street to begin his daily activities. Donning an eye-catching diamond ring, he had earned himself the nickname "Diamond Dick." Little did he know what would unfold within this town as he rang for the elevator that day.

Sara Page, a 17-year-old white girl from Kansas City, worked as an elevator operator. One day, Dick Rowland entered her elevator and stumbled as it jolted unexpectedly, accidentally brushing against Sara. Startled, she screamed, drawing the attention of a white clerk nearby. Panicking, Dick immediately fled the scene. The following morning, Dick Rowland was arrested and accused of attempting to assault and rape Sara Page. The Tulsa Tribune covered the story, portraying Sara Page as an orphan trying to pay for her education. However, when questioned by authorities, Sara Page revised her statement and chose not to press charges. Unfortunately, an angry mob had already assembled outside the courthouse.

To safeguard Dick Rowland, a group of prominent Black leaders marched toward the courthouse to confront the enraged mob. Among them were younger Black men, including war veterans, who arrived armed with guns and ammunition as a show of solidarity. Chaos erupted when a white man tried to snatch a revolver from a young Black man, causing it to go off. This incident sparked a deadly exchange of gunfire among the crowd, resulting in further conflicts spreading back to Greenwood.

The National Guard was summoned for support, and around 500 white men were deputized in response, many Klansmen. These deputies were given free rein to kill any "nigger" they encountered, granting them permission for murder. With anticipation building up until daybreak, the mob turned their jealousy-fueled rage into action by storming through Greenwood, looting homes, and setting buildings ablaze one by one.

A massive white mob of around 20,000 people swarmed in from neighboring cities, taking matters into their own hands. They wrought havoc on Greenwood, demolishing businesses, churches, and stores and setting homes ablaze. Meanwhile, the National Guard launched air attacks with dynamite and mounted machine guns. Countless innocent individuals were either rounded up or shot while trying to escape. Amidst this chaos, about 6,000 African Americans were forcefully marched out of Greenwood at gunpoint as white families observed nearby, some even posing for pictures.

Discover the captivating story of O.W. Gurley, the visionary founder behind the legendary Greenwood, famously known as Black Wall Street. Back in July 1906, Gurley made a life-changing decision, setting his sights on Tulsa and acquiring a remarkable 40-acre plot of land. However, this land was destined for a groundbreaking purpose - it would be exclusively sold to African Americans. Thus, Gurley's bold vision was set in motion.

As the dust settled near the bustling railroad tracks, Gurley opened his first business, a modest yet welcoming rooming house. Located on a dusty trail that he dubbed Greenwood, in honor of a city in Arkansas, this humble establishment quickly became a haven for those seeking refuge from the oppressive conditions prevailing in Mississippi. Migrants found solace in the rooms Gurley provided, situated conveniently near the Frisco railroad tracks.

But Gurley's ambitions didn't stop there. Together with his wife, Emma, he embarked on an impressive journey of construction and development. They built three magnificent two-story buildings, alongside five residences, showcasing their dedication to the growth of Greenwood. Additionally, their ventures extended beyond the city limits, as they invested in an expansive 80-acre farm located in Rogers County.

Not far from Gurley's pursuits, another influential figure emerged - J.B. Stradford. Born in Versailles, Kentucky, to an enslaved father, Stradford triumphed over his humble origins, driven by an unyielding determination. Armed with an education from Oberlin College and a law degree from Indiana Law School, he established himself as a prominent Black businessman and accomplished lawyer. Stradford played an instrumental role in the development of Greenwood, acquiring vast tracts of land north of the Frisco railroad tracks.

However, despite the initial success and prosperity, tragedy struck Greenwood with devastating force. The race war of

1921 dealt a heavy blow to Gurley's prominence and wealth, leaving him with nothing. The iconic Gurley Hotel, located at 112 N. Greenwood, served as the street's inaugural commercial enterprise, valued at an impressive $55,000. Within its walls, the vibrant Brunswick Billiard Parlor and the beloved Dock Eastmand & Hughes Cafe found their home. Sadly, all were reduced to ruins, lost in the ravages of the conflict. Additionally, Gurley owned a two-story building at 119 N. Greenwood, housing Carter's Barbershop, Hardy Rooms, a pool hall, and a cherished cigar store, all of which suffered the same fate.

According to Gurley's own account and court records, the toll of the 1921 race war was staggering. Nearly $200,000, a fortune in those times, slipped through his fingers, leaving him to grapple with the profound loss.

Thus, the legacy of O.W. Gurley and the resilience of Black Wall Street are intricately woven into the fabric of history. It stands as a testament to the indomitable spirit of those who dared to dream and the enduring strength of a community that refused to be silenced.

CIVIL RIGHTS STRUGGLES, SACRIFICE, AND EQUALITY

In 1936, African Americans shifted their support from the Republican Party to Franklin D. Roosevelt, who was running for president. They greatly respected Roosevelt for his strong stance on civil rights. In 1941, he established the Fair Employment Practices Committee (FEPC) through an executive order banning discrimination based on race, color, religion, or nationality. Additionally, Roosevelt initiated a program that enabled 50,000 Black farmers to access government loans and set up a federal minimum wage. Eleanor Roosevelt, his wife, made headlines when she resigned from the Daughters of the American Revolution (DAR) after they denied African American singer Marian Anderson from performing at Constitutional Hall in Washington, D.C., due to her race. Subsequently, Eleanor helped organize a concert for Anderson at the Lincoln Memorial on Easter Sunday – an iconic event attended by over 75,000 people.

On April 12, 1945, Harry S. Truman stepped into the spotlight as he was sworn in as America's President, succeeding Franklin D. Roosevelt after his sudden death. Truman rose to fame with impressive accomplishments – defeating Nazi Germany, establishing NATO, and founding the United Nations. However, his decision to prioritize civil rights made him one of the nation's most controversial presidents. Truman had once considered himself a bigot, but witnessing violence against veterans by white supremacists sparked a change within him. He made history as the first president to address the NAACP, promising to tackle Jim Crow laws, abolish poll taxes, and fight job discrimination. This bold stand on civil rights caused many Southerners, known as Dixiecrats, to abandon the Democratic Party.

Undeterred, President Truman called on Congress to pass legislation that would dismantle the KKK and challenge states' rights to stamp out Klan-related violence. Truman's unwavering commitment reshaped America's political landscape and prioritized civil rights as a national issue.

In January 1957, Dr. Martin Luther King took charge of the Southern Christian Leadership Conference, advocating for nonviolent social change and uniting various civil rights organizations. As a Baptist minister in Montgomery's Dexter Avenue Baptist Church, Dr. King got involved in civil rights battles after learning about Rosa Parks. She was an NAACP officer and seamstress who defied a city law demanding that Black people surrender their bus seats for white passengers. One incident involved a white man who declined to sit beside a Black person, prompting the bus driver to insist for Parks to vacate her seat. This resulted in her arrest and led to the Montgomery Improvement Association (MIA) boycott in 1955. Dr. King was chosen as MIA's president and fought against racial segregation on public transport for 381 days. During this time, the homes of Dr. King and Dr. Ralph Abernathy were bombed, with both leaders being arrested. Their dedication ultimately paid off – the city repealed the discriminatory law, and the U.S. Supreme Court declared segregated public seating unconstitutional in December 1956.

The Montgomery Bus Boycott emerged as the first united demonstration in the South, despite encountering aggression from white supremacist factions targeting Black leaders and churches orchestrating the protests. Black-owned businesses and religious institutions were devastated by dynamite amidst the uproar.

On September 15, 1963, a fateful morning at the 16th Street Baptist Church in Birmingham, Alabama, a bomb detonated beneath the staircase, tragically claiming the lives of four young girls and becoming a crucial moment in the Civil Rights Movement. Before that, Reverend George Lee and Lamar Smith were fatally shot for their efforts to partake in Mississippi's voting process, occurring just two months before the horrific demise of Emmitt Till.

Theophilus Eugene "Bull" Connor, the commissioner of public safety for Birmingham, promised the streets would run red with blood before the city of Birmingham allowed integration. Connors ordered fire hoses and attack dogs against the Freedom Riders and conspired with Klansmen to brutally beat African Americans during the demonstration. The drama unfolded with President John F. Kennedy denouncing the cruelty of segregation and offering support for the protesters from across the nation.

During the 1950s and '60s, Blacks were targeted by police for protesting, but the desire for equality overpowered the status quo maintaining white supremacy. Across the South, some protests were successful in denouncing segregation. However, many martyrs were mourned in the process. Atrocities in America have always been honest, and gaining freedom was just as painful as war.

On a fateful day, August 28, 1955, 14-year-old Emmett Till met his tragic end after allegedly uttering "Bye, baby" to Carolyn Bryant, a 21-year-old white woman in Money, Mississippi. Carolyn married Roy Bryant, who owned a small grocery store called Bryant's Grocery. Emmett was staying at a relative's house when Roy and his half-brother, John Milam, forcefully took him from the house.

Medger Evers and NAACP field officers from Jackson, Mississippi, joined forces to search for Emmett Till. Brave Black witnesses eventually stepped forward and shared vital information about the incident. Emmett's lifeless body was found in the Tallahatchie River three days later with a 70-pound cotton gin fan attached to his neck by barbed wire.

He had suffered a gunshot to the head, lost an eye, and his skull was crushed. His battered body returned to Chicago, where his mother demanded a public funeral with an open casket, allowing the world to witness the gruesome reality of Emmett's death. At the trial, Emmitt's uncle, Morris Wright, bravely testified and accused the defendants of murder.

However, the conspirators were acquitted amidst laughter in the courtroom. Later, killers Roy Bryant and John Milam confessed to the crime in a magazine interview, shamelessly boasting about their actions. This demonstrated how white supremacy allowed the legal system to mock African Americans seeking justice.

Upon returning from World War II, Medgar Evers dove headfirst into the Civil Rights Movement. Despite completing his education at Alcorn State University, he faced the harsh reality of discrimination when his application to the University of Mississippi Law School in 1954 was denied. This experience underscored the obstacles black individuals encountered while pursuing a better life. On a tragic night, June 11, 1963, Evers was fatally shot in front of his young children by a white supremacist named Byron Beck. A year later, another heartbreaking incident occurred on June 21, 1964. James Chaney, a young Black civil rights worker, and two white workers—Andrew Goodman and Michael Schwerner—were mercilessly killed during a sponsored voter registration drive. After being arrested for speeding and released by local deputies, the trio fell into the hands of murderous Klansmen. During Freedom Summer, their lifeless bodies were later discovered in the Tallahaga Dam close to Philadelphia, Neshoba County, Mississippi.

That same year, white supremacist groups set fire to nearly 40 churches amidst Freedom Summer as the FBI illegally wiretapped and broke into Reverend Martin Luther King's property. Simultaneously, Africa encountered comparable turmoil under the apartheid caste system. European powers effectively employed the Aryan caste method to separate communities that had once coexisted harmoniously, intermarrying and living as peaceful neighbors.

For instance, Europeans exploited deception and the lighter complexion of the Tutsis to create divisions among African people. By granting special privileges to Tutsis over Hutus, Europeans incited internal ethnic discord among East Africans. Capitalizing on this cultural rift, Belgium and France introduced identity cards indicating ethnic origin, solidifying a perpetual racial divide between the two groups.

CHAPTER ELEVEN

The Historical Narratives of Rwanda, Burundi, and South Africa in the Eyes of Ezekiel

Before World War I, Rwanda and Burundi were colonized by Germany and Belgium, which utilized minority Tutsis in education and politics as a regulatory tactic. Though a late arrival to the African colonization game, Germany adopted the same damaging strategies of deception used by other European nations, pitting racially related African groups against one another and disrupting their culture. In 1959, Belgium extended political participation to the Hutu majority through elections and dismantled the Tutsi Monarchy in favor of a republican leadership model. By 1962, Belgium transferred power to a smaller Tutsi population in Burundi and granted independence to Rwanda with Hutus at the helm. As these two African countries gained independence, political and social tensions between ethnic factions intensified, resulting in decades of violence.

The Hutus claimed that the highly educated Tutsis aimed to subjugate the majority Hutu population, intensifying ethnic friction. In 1990, Tutsi refugees from Uganda and Burundi stormed northern Rwanda to curb the ruling Hutu government, igniting ethnic genocide and sparking civil wars fueled by European colonists' discriminatory divide-and-conquer tactics. On April 6, 1994, peace negotiations stopped when a plane carrying the presidents of Rwanda and Burundi was brought down.

In April 1994, heavily armed United Nations forces landed in Rwanda to escort European and American civilians out of the country, leaving the Tutsi population defenseless. Determined to slaughter every Tutsi in Rwanda, the Hutus targeted women, children, and dissenting Hutus. When Paul Kagame triumphed in July 1994 and signed a peace treaty in 1995, over 800,000 Tutsis were killed, millions fled for shelter in neighboring countries, and the world they have remained silent. Though divided by ethnicity, Tutsis and Hutus once shared a common language, traditions, and religion. They even intermarried. Most of the population consisted of Hutus more than 80%, mainly farmers. Due to European settlers' favoritism, the Tutsis were largely cattle herders who grew wealthier and more educated than their Hutu counterparts.

During the same period, South Africa implemented apartheid - a legal system of racial segregation classifying its citizens into a hierarchy. The British and Dutch colonized the region in the 17th century, and when the National Party gained power in 1948, they reinforced the caste system to uphold white supremacy. This system controlled every aspect of Black Africans' lives and prohibited interracial marriages.

Black communities were shifted from urban to rural tribal zones to guarantee isolation. Numerous Blacks were compelled to work in agriculture and mining, often separated from their families due to the remote locations of these worksites. The government seized their land and allocated it to white people. Native Africans, facing limited options, worked unfavorable jobs to earn a livelihood while enduring racism and oppression. In some cases, Black-owned farms were razed, leading to food deprivation and forcing them into tribal camps. Many who resisted apartheid succumbed to malnutrition or illness as access to medical care or basic hygiene was restricted.

In 1951, the Prevention of Illegal Squatting Act aimed to evict Black individuals residing in white neighborhoods forcibly. The subsequent year, the Abolition of Pass Act mandated all Africans to have a single passbook in white areas. This pass unveiled one's race, job, and current address and was necessary to enter a white neighborhood. Originating from a 1760 law that required enslaved people to carry a pass, this updated "super pass" consolidated all documents into one folder. By 1950, all South Africans had to register under the Population Registration Act and were categorized into four racial groups: white, Indian, colored, or Black. Black people were at the bottom of this hierarchy and forced always to carry a pass. This cruel treatment sparked protests throughout South Africa as the Apartheid government supported continued discrimination.

In 1960, organizations such as the African National Congress (ANC) and Pan Africanist Congress (PAC) rallied for a peaceful protest against this law and advocated for political change in Sharpeville. On March 21st of that year, a massive gathering—including PAC leader Robert Sobukwe— surrounded a police station in defiance of the passed law. The police reacted by firing into the crowd, killing 69 people and injuring over 200 others. Robert Sobukwe was arrested, and other protests supporting anti-apartheid took place throughout several South African towns, with thousands participating.

In response to the rising protests, the South African government implemented the Ninety Day Act, granting law enforcement the power to arrest anyone suspected of anti-government activities. As the brutality grew, South Africa severed ties with its largest trading partner, the British Commonwealth, and became a Republic. Both parties couldn't maintain their economic relationship despite their shared interest in gold and diamonds.

Following the devastating Sharpeville Massacre, the ANC and PAC formed military wings – Umkhonto we Sizwe (Spear of the Nation) and Poqo (we go alone) – to fight against apartheid. These wings underwent guerilla training in other African countries like Ghana, Tanzania, and Zambia to prepare for combat against the oppressive apartheid government. South Africa's government struck back on April 8, 1960, by banning the ANC and PAC under a State of Emergency Act that prohibited public gatherings. Nelson Mandela spearheaded Umkhonto's efforts by orchestrating sabotage missions on white-ruled structures and communication systems to resist the minority-led regime.

There was growing pressure from the global community to halt investments and trade with the apartheid regime. Foreign athletes joined the cause by boycotting sporting events. The world finally started confronting the horrendous conditions in South African squatter settlements. On August 5, 1962, Nelson Mandela was captured near Howie Falls en route to Johannesburg, reportedly due to a CIA tip-off. The following year, other ANC leaders were arrested while plotting against the apartheid government at Liliesleaf Farm in Rivonia, South Africa.

During the 1964 Rivonia Treason Trial, eight anti-apartheid activists, including Mandela, received life imprisonment.

On June 16, 1976, about 20,000 students from Soweto near Johannesburg staged a peaceful protest against discriminatory education policies. Police met them with tear gas and gunfire. This triggered riots, now known as the Soweto Uprising, which led to hundreds of African youth fatalities. While the official death count is 176, the actual number could be as high as 700.

A year after the uprising, on August 18, Steve Biko was detained at a police checkpoint under Terrorism Act 83. Biko led the Black Conscious Movement and organized the Soweto Uprising. This movement was outlawed by the Apartheid Government in 1973. During questioning, Biko faced unimaginable brutality; he was shackled to a window grille and beaten naked, suffering a severe brain injury. He tragically passed away en route to Pretoria Prison.

By 1989, de Klerk made a daring move by lifting the ban on the ANC and 32 other groups, vowing to satisfy the majority's demands by freeing Nelson Mandela from his cell. Global pressure to sever business ties with South Africa's government only intensified as the boycott started to cripple the apartheid regime. In 1990, F.W. de Klerk kept his word and authorized Nelson Mandela's release after 27 long years behind bars, along with other political detainees.

A historic moment arrived in April 1994 when South Africa held its first democratic elections, propelling Nelson Mandela to the presidency and making the ANC the country's dominant political force.

[7] *"For a mere moment I have forsaken you,*
But with great mercies I will gather you.
[8] *With a little wrath I hid My face from you for a moment;*
But with everlasting kindness I will have mercy on you...
[13] *All your children shall be taught by the Lord,*

And great shall be the peace of your children.

[14] In righteousness you shall be established;

You shall be far from oppression, for you shall not fear;

And from terror, for it shall not come near you.

[15] Indeed they shall surely assemble, but not because of Me.

Whoever assembles against you shall fall for your sake.

[17] No weapon formed against you shall prosper, And every tongue which

rises against you in judgment You shall condemn...

(New King James Version, Isaiah 54:7-8, 13-15, 17)

DIVINE JUDGMENTS AND PROPHETIC WARNINGS

The story of Ezekiel begins with him experiencing vivid, symbolic visions while he is held captive near the Chebar River, southeast of Babylon. He shares his awe as the heavens open up and reveal divine visions. In 597 BC., at just 25 years old, Ezekiel was taken captive by Nebuchadnezzar during the second invasion of Jerusalem. Alongside approximately 3,000 upper-class citizens, he lived in Tel Abib, a foreign land. Here, five years later, Ezekiel was called to become a prophet.

On the tragic day of Jerusalem's final siege, Ezekiel was struck by a personal revelation—his beloved wife would be taken from him instantly. However, even in his grief, he was instructed not to mourn or weep for her loss (24:16). In his initial symbolic vision, Ezekiel witnessed a massive whirlwind emerging from the north, accompanied by a fiery cloud encircled by a glowing aura. Within this scene, he spotted four human-like creatures, each possessing an ox's face on one side and an eagle's visage on the other, along with two sets of wings.

These creatures appeared bright as burning coals and had hands hidden beneath their wings. Above these peculiar beings loomed a crystalline expanse that spanned overhead. Perched atop this canopy was what seemed to be a sapphire throne. Cherubim, heavenly creatures, descended and were encircled by a blazing, amber-colored rainbow. This astonishing sight left Ezekiel awe-struck, causing him to fall face-first onto the ground.

Then, a divine entity ordered Ezekiel to rise and helped him to his feet. The Spirit of the Lord went on to share a message with Ezekiel:

> ³ *And He said to me: "Son of man, I am sending you to the children of Israel,*
>
> *to a rebellious nation that has rebelled against Me;*
>
> *they and their fathers have transgressed against Me to this very day.*
>
> ⁴ *For they are impudent and stubborn children.*
>
> *I am sending you to them, and you shall say to them,*
>
> *'Thus says the Lord God.'*
>
> ⁵ *As for them, whether they hear or whether they refuse--for they are a rebellious house--yet they will know that a prophet has been among them.*
>
> *(New King James Version, Ezekiel 2:3-5)*

Ezekiel's prophecies unveil divine judgments upon Judah and neighboring covenant nations, such as Ammon, Moab, Tyre, Sidon, Edom, Egypt, and Ethiopia. Their acceptance of idolatry and refusal to embrace their firstborn status provoked God's wrath, leaving no room for mercy. As firstborns, they were supposed to enjoy special rights and spiritual privileges with God.

[13] All the firstborn of man among your sons you shall redeem. So, it shall be when your son asks you in time to come, saying, "What is this?" That you shall say to him, "By strength of hand the Lord brought us out of the house of bondage."

(New King James Version, Exodus 13:13)

Ezekiel continues with his prophecy:

You have feared the sword, and I will bring a sword upon you, says the Lord God. And I will bring out of its midst, deliver you into the hands of strangers, and execute judgments on you...

I will do these things to you because you have gone as a harlot after the Gentiles because you have become defiled by their idols. You have walked in the way of your sister; therefore, I will put her cup in your hand. In a remarkable shift, power transitioned from the Hebrews to the Gentiles, who were previously unfamiliar with the Creator God Yahweh. The Hebrews started to discover a God overflowing with love and forgiveness, readily pardoning sins upon true repentance and possessing a fierce aspect. As many Hebrews married foreigners and embraced their shady religions, they were cautioned against adopting Pagan deities. The prophecy continued:

[3] ....It will be a day of clouds, the time of the Gentiles.

[4] The sword shall come upon Egypt, And great anguish shall be in Ethiopia...

[5] "Ethiopia, Libya, Lydia, all the mingled people, Chub, and the men of the lands who are allied, shall fall with them by the sword."

(New King James Version, Ezekiel 30:4-6)

Throughout history, powerful kingdoms rose and will rule until the Lord's second coming. The book of Luke describes how the Hebrews fell under the control of these formidable Pagan nations.

> [24] *And they will fall by the edge of the sword,*
> *and be led away captive into all nations.*
> *And Jerusalem will be trampled by Gentiles*
> *until the times of the Gentiles are fulfilled.*
> [27] *Then they will see the Son of Man coming*
> *in a cloud with power and great glory.*
>
> *(New King James Version,* Luke 21:24, 27)

Ezekiel's compelling vision of restoration started with the stunning Vision of Dry Bones. Divinely guided, he ventured through a valley where he saw a glimpse of Israel's destiny. Fleeing from Nebuchadnezzar's siege on Jerusalem, numerous Jews took refuge in Upper Egypt. In contrast, others disregarded Prophet Jeremiah's counsel and settled in an Egyptian region called Pathros, now a part of northern Sudan and among the world's most impoverished areas. In this extraordinary vision, Ezekiel saw bones reassemble into complete skeletons as ligaments, flesh, and skin revived them. They even began to quiver but remained lifeless. Eventually, these once-dead bones morphed into a powerful human army. They expressed their despair as they felt disconnected from the House of Israel with their dry bones and vanished hope.

Providing faith to them, Ezekiel was divinely commanded to prophesy: "Thus says the Lord God: 'Behold, O My people, I will open your graves and cause you to come up from your graves, and bring you into the land of Israel. Then you shall know that I am the Lord'" (Ezekiel 37). Prophet Zephaniah assured that the Lord would preserve a remnant of people. Fulfilling this prophecy, Ethiopia lost territories to foreigners but managed to avoid colonization. Numerous Ethiopians remained loyal servants, and the prophet encouraged the Hebrew people to reunite with the Lord.

At the beginning of Zephaniah's vision, he proclaimed a judgment on Ethiopians and Israelites alike, yet ended on a hopeful note with a promise of restoration in the following text.

> [9] *"For then I will restore to the peoples a pure language,*
> *That they all may call on the name of the Lord, To serve Him with one accord.*
> [10] *From beyond the rivers of Ethiopia My worshipers,*
> *The daughter of My dispersed ones…*
> [11] *In that day you shall not be shamed for any of your deeds*
> *In which you transgress against Me; For then I will take away*
> *from your midst Those who rejoice in your pride…*
> [20] *At that time I will bring you back, Even at the time I gather you;*
> *For I will give you fame and praise Among all the peoples of the earth,*
> *When I return your captives before your eyes,"*
> *(New King James Version, Zephaniah 3:10-11, 20)*

In the year that King Uzziah of Judah passed away, Isaiah experienced his first divine vision. He witnessed the Lord seated on a magnificent throne, with His glorious presence and the brilliance of His robe filling the entire temple. Seraphim, heavenly beings with six wings each, hovered above the throne. The door's supporting columns shook as an angel's voice resounded, and the temple became shrouded in smoke. Isaiah told the Lord, "Woe is me, for I am undone! Because I am a man of unclean lips, and I dwell among a people of unclean lips; for my eyes have seen the King, The Lord of hosts."

Then the seraphim touched Isaiah's mouth with a hot coal from the altar and said, "Behold, this has touched your lips; your iniquity is taken away, and your sin purged." In a divine vision, God revealed to Isaiah that his mission would be one of judgment. Due to their unfaithfulness, the Hebrew people would be forsaken by the Lord and deemed outcasts. The Gentiles' influence had tainted Israel, Judah, and the entire Cushite region, turning it into a hotbed for religious betrayal and idolatry. Despite the prophets' relentless harsh warnings and pleas, the Hebrews could not resist the allure of the Gentiles' materialism and seductive ways.

The writer of Deuteronomy foresaw and shared an impending prophecy of retribution for the Hebrew people:

[20] *"The Lord will send on you cursing, confusion,*
and rebuke in all that you set your hand to do...
[24] *The Lord will change the rain of your land to powder and dust;*
from the heaven it shall come down on you until you are destroyed.
[25] *The Lord will cause you to be defeated before your enemies;*
you shall go out one way against them and flee seven ways before them;
and you shall become troublesome to all the kingdoms of the earth.
[48] *therefore you shall serve your enemies, whom the Lord will send against*
you, in hunger, in thirst, in nakedness, and in need of everything; and
He will put a yoke of iron on your neck until He has destroyed you.
(New King James Version, Deuteronomy 28: 20, 24-25, 48)

The Mediterranean Coastline's residents witnessed a heart-pounding series of events as the Jewish people suffered defeat after defeat at the hands of the Babylonians. The attack came swiftly, and casualties mounted during a brutal invasion that extended into Cushite lands. During this turmoil, the prophet Habakkuk questioned the Lord's intentions.

"O Lord, You have appointed them for judgment... Why do you look on those who deal treacherously, and hold Your tongue when the wicked devours a person more righteous than he?"

At last, the prophet Habakkuk received word of their mightiest allies along the Nile facing plunder and being forced to pay a big tribute to Babylon: "I saw the tents of the Cushan in affliction; the curtains of the land of Midian trembled." Upon hearing news of the horrifying invasion by Babylonian, Chaldean, and Scythian forces conquering lands throughout the Mediterranean and Egyptian coast, Habakkuk started voicing his "Cry for Justice" to the Lord. The Babylonians were ruthless and craved material riches. Intriguingly, they shared historical ties with Balkan immigrants and joined forces with scattered Assyrian and Scythian tribes to pursue imperialism, spreading their toxic influence further along the Nile Delta.

The sacred bond was broken as Babylonian forces advanced toward the Jewish kingdom, launching a fierce campaign of destruction and turmoil. Instead of praying for victory over the Scythian and Babylonian armies, the prophet mourned his people's hatred and sinful deeds. Habakkuk's grievances and inquiries led to visions that evoked both sorrowful and consoling prophecies. In the book's opening chapter, named after him, he receives a revelation that God was employing the Babylonians as a means of judgment against those who broke the covenant.

[6] For indeed I am raising up the Chaldeans,
A bitter and hasty nation Which marches through the breadth of the earth,
To possess dwelling places that are not theirs.
[7] They are terrible and dreadful;
Their judgment and their dignity proceed from themselves.

⁸ Their horses also are swifter than leopards,

And more fierce than evening wolves...

⁹...They gather captives like sand.

¹¹...He commits offense, ascribing this power to his god.

(New King James Version, Habakkuk 1:6-9,11*)*

In Isaiah's captivating story, God instructed him to walk naked and barefooted for three years, serving as a distinct symbol for Egypt and Ethiopia. The Hebrews, a chosen and unique group, shone like a guiding light for the Gentile world.

"I will also give you as a light to the Gentiles; you should be My salvation to the ends of the earth" (Isaiah 49:6). Curious, Isaiah sought guidance from the Lord, wondering the length of time people must endure suffering. The Lord responded with a foreboding message: suffering would persist until cities become desolate, devoid of life. With Judah relying on the Cushites for protection, Isaiah urgently reminded his fellow Jewish people that only God could be their true savior. This dire prophecy prophesied destruction not just for Judah but also for Egypt and Ethiopia. Coinciding with this ominous prediction, Ezekiel foresaw a devastating famine in Ethiopia. "Indeed, therefore, I am against you and your rivers, and I will make the land of Egypt utterly waste and desolate, from Migdol to Syene, as far as the border of Ethiopia" (Ezekiel 29:10).

ISAIAH AND REVELATION'S VISIONS OF RESTORATION AND JUDGMENT

Isaiah's vision unfolds, shifting focus towards the judgment of the Gentiles and the renewal of Jewish and African communities. "Descend and sit amidst the dust, O pure Babylon; take your seat on the ground, throneless, O child of Chaldeans!" Drawing parallels to the book of Revelation, this passage might represent the same judgment enacted as the lamb opened each of the seven seals, unleashing a sequence of catastrophes upon the Gentiles.

> [6] *I was angry with My people; I have profaned My inheritance,*
> *And given them into your hand. You showed them no mercy;*
> *On the elderly you laid your yoke very heavily.*
> [7] *And you said, 'I shall be a lady forever,'*
> *So that you did not take these things to heart,*
> *Nor remember the latter end of them.*
> [10] *You have said, 'No one sees me';*
> *Your wisdom and your knowledge have warped you;*
>
> *(New King James Version, Isaiah 47:1-11)*

And;

> [8] ..."*In an acceptable time I have heard You, And in the day of salvation I have helped You; I will preserve You and give You As a covenant to the people, To restore the earth...*
> [15] "*Can a woman forget her nursing child,*
> *And not have compassion on the son of her womb?...*
> [26] *I will feed those who oppress you with their own flesh, And they shall be drunk with their own blood as with sweet wine. All flesh shall know That I, the Lord, am your Savior, And your Redeemer, the Mighty One of Jacob.*"
>
> *(New King James Version, Isaiah 49:8, 15, 26)*

In Isaiah, chapter 60, the prophet shares a captivating prophecy detailing the rejuvenation of the Israelites and African people.

*¹Arise; shine; for your light has come! And the glory of the Lord is risen upon you. ²For behold, the darkness shall cover the earth, and deep darkness the people…⁶the multitude of camels shall cover the land, and the dromedaries of **Midian** and **Ephah**; all those from **Sheba** shall come; they shall bring gold and incense, and they shall proclaim the praises of the Lord.*

(New King James Version, Isaiah 60: 1-2, 6)

Imagine a thriving oasis, bustling with life, as the Sahara and Aswan deserts transform from barren wastelands to flourishing landscapes with meandering rivers and vibrant communities.

³The Gentiles will come to your light. And the kings to the brightness of your rising…⁵then you will become radiant, and your heart will swell with joy; because the abundance of the sea shall be returned to you, the wealth of the Gentiles shall come to you.

(New King James Version, Isaiah 60:3, 5)

Isaiah, the prophet, was granted a thrilling peek into the future, where he witnessed remarkable events unfolding in the imminent messianic era. He saw diverse people from various ethnicities united in worshipping the Son of God. The vision also vividly displayed Africa's landscape and left no room for doubt that Israel would enjoy a bountiful resurgence in economic prosperity.

¹⁰For in My wrath, I struck you, but in My favor, I have had mercy on you. ¹¹Therefore, your gates shall be open continually; they shall not be shut day or night that men may bring to you the wealth of the Gentiles.¹² For the nation and kingdom which will not serve you shall perish, and these nations shall be utterly ruined.

(New King James Version, Isaiah 60:10-12*)*

Along with the amazing gifts of the Afrocentric world, they'd receive twice the recognition and a cause for celebration in their homeland. The storm of chaos would finally subside as people of African heritage bid farewell to the Western world and journey back to their ancestral lands.

> *9And the ships of Tarshish will comes [sic] first, to bring your sons from afar, their silver and gold with them, to the name of the Lord your God...14Also the sons of those who afflicted you shall come bowing to you, and all who despised you shall fall and prostrate at the soles of your feet.*
>
> *(New King James Version, Isaiah 60:9-14)*

> *9Indeed, I will make those of the synagogue of Satan, who say they are Jews and are not, but lie indeed I will make them come and worship before your feet, and to know that I have loved you...17Because you say, "I am rich, have become wealthy, and have need of nothing, and do not know that you are wretched, miserable, poor, blind and naked."*
>
> *(New King James Version, Revelation 3:9,17)*

During his exile on the island of Patmos, John experienced a divine encounter with Yeshua the Christ, who revealed a series of vivid, metaphorical visions to him. These captivating glimpses foretold the dramatic conclusion of the Time of the Gentiles, seen through John's eyes while on the island. In enthralling chapter 17, John is transported into the wilderness by one of the seven angels. Here, he witnesses a staggering sight - a woman, intoxicated and covered in the blood of Christ's martyrs, riding atop a seven-headed dragon. This woman symbolizes the mighty city of Babylon, which held sway over all earthly kings.

Suddenly, an angel pours his bowl into the air and, with a thundering voice that booms from heaven, declares, "It is done!" The world quakes as John hears the noisy rumbles of an earthquake accompanied by thunderclaps and bright lightning flashes. God now remembers Babylon's mysteries and unleashes His fierce wrath. He tears apart this once-great nation into three distinct pieces. During this vision, John watches mountains crumble to dust, hail rain down from heaven, and islands shift from their original locations.

The intrigued angel then asks John why he is so astonished and explains the deeper meaning behind this jaw-dropping vision.

> [9]*Here is the mind which has wisdom: The seven heads are sevens mountains on which the woman sits.* [10]*There are also seven kings. Five has fallen, one is, and the other has not come. And when he comes, he must continue a short time.* [11]*The beast that was, and is not, is himself also the eighth, and is of the seven, and is going to perdition…*[13]*these are one mind. And they will give their power and authority to the beast.*
> *(New King James Version, Revelation 17: 9-11, 13))*

In chapter 18 of the book of Revelation, John witnesses a powerful angel proclaiming Babylon's destruction. John's vision portrays the angel as a divine messenger, emanating great authority and representing the heavenly realm. The illumination of the earth with the angel's glory symbolizes the revelation of a profound spiritual truth. The angel's cry highlights the monumental collapse of Babylon, a symbolic representation of an evil and influential entity. Babylon's fall signifies the ultimate judgment and destruction of a corrupt and immoral system.

To sum it up, Revelation 18 tells the tale of Babylon's downfall, which symbolizes a corrupt system that has fallen into ruin and become a home for demons and a sign of spiritual contamination. This eye-opening vision warns us about the dire repercussions of indulging in immoral behavior and highlights the inevitable judgment awaiting everything that defies God's ethical standards. For all nations have drunk of the wine of the wrath of her fornication, the kings of the earth have committed fornication with her, and the merchants of the world have become rich through the abundance of her luxury. Let's take a closer look at the inspiring words from the book of Isaiah, "Arise and shine, for your light has arrived!" Similarly, pay attention to the captivating verses John heard with a similar message:

> *⁴Come out of her, my people, lest you share in her sins, and lest you receive of her plagues. ⁵For her sins have reached to heaven, and God has remembered her iniquities. ⁶Render to her just as she rendered to you, and repay her double according to her works, in the cup which she mixed, mix double for her...*
>
> *(New King James Version, Revelation 18:4-6)*

In the measure that she glorified herself and lived luxuriously, in the same measure give her torment and sorrow; for she says in her heart, "I sit as queen, and am no widow, and will not see sorrow. Therefore, her plagues will come in one day-death, mourning, and famine. And she will be utterly burned with fire, for strong is the Lord God who judges her.

> *¹"Behold! My Servant whom I uphold, My elect One in whom My soul delights! I have put My Spirit upon Him; He will bring justice to the Gentiles. ²He will not cry out nor raise His voice...³He will bring forth justice for truth. ⁴He will not fall nor be discouraged, till He has established justice in the earth; and the coastlands shall wait for His law."*
>
> *(New King James Version, Isaiah 42:1-4)*

In this captivating excerpt from the Bible (Matthew 24:6-8), Yeshua the Christ responds to his disciples' curiosity about the indicators of his return and the conclusion of an era. He highlights particular events and phenomena that signify the approaching end times. The passage suggests widespread geopolitical unrest, and conflicts, along with resource scarcity leading to societal and economic turmoil, will be a common sight. The emergence of wars, famines, and earthquakes are informative signs of the nearing fulfillment of biblical prophecies and the ultimate climax of human history.

> *[6]You will hear of wars and rumors of wars, for all these things must come to pass, but the end is not yet. [7]Nation will rise against nations, and kingdom against kingdom. And there will be famines, pestilences, and earthquakes in various places; [8]all these things are the beginning of sorrows…[21]For then there will be great tribulation, such as has not been since the beginning of the world until this time, no, nor ever shall be. [22]And unless those days were shortened, no flesh would be saved; but for the elect's sake those days will be shortened.*
>
> *(New King James Version, Matthew 24:6-8, 21-22)*

Conversion of Paul, Idolatry Warning, and Spiritual Warfare

Over two decades after Christ's ministry, Apostle Paul experienced a transformation and dedicated the rest of his life to spreading the message of Christ's Second Coming. Once tasked by the high priest to apprehend Christ's followers, Paul and historian Josephus believed that God had ordained Romans to rule over Israelites as they too were Roman citizens. This sense of superiority often led to greater loyalty towards those in power, but Paul broke free from this perplexing devotion to the caste system after Christ's influence on him.

In 66 A.D., amidst the Jewish-Roman War sparked during Nero's reign, Josephus was appointed as Galilee's governor when Jews revolted. Many Jewish leaders deemed Josephus a traitor due to his excessive political clout. Despite belonging to the Jewish priesthood and royalty, Josephus proclaimed doom upon Jews after his capture by the Romans, believing it to be God's will. After Emperor Nero's suicide in 68 AD., Vespasian ascended as emperor while his son Titus led the Jewish War. In 70 AD., over a million Jews perished for not succumbing to Roman rule, and Vespasian commanded their forts to be destroyed.

Paul had once been pro-Roman and indifferent towards his people, even persecuting early Gospel followers before his faith in Christ emerged. Romans ruled remotely by employing native rulers and Roman advisors while exploiting Hebrew resources under a manipulative illusion. However, Apostle Paul renounced such teachings after Yeshua the Christ converted him and chose him as a beacon of light for Gentiles. Post-conversion, Paul argued that religious leaders did a disservice to Gentiles by not revealing the falsehoods of these deities. In 1 Corinthians 10:14-20, Paul passionately warns believers to steer clear of idolatry, underlining the spiritual consequences that come with it. He inspires clarity and wisdom, emphasizing the difference between lifeless idols and the worship of the one and only true God.

The core message of this passage is quite simple: Idolatry goes beyond just worshipping inanimate objects; it's intertwined with a dark spiritual reality. The sacrifices made by Gentiles aren't for God but for demons. So, believers should avoid engaging in idolatrous practices to avoid entangled with demonic forces. Addressing the Corinthians as "wise men," Paul urges them to use sound judgment and discernment. He asks whether there's any importance in an idol or its offerings. His response clarifies that idols don't possess power or divinity alone. Engaging in idolatry inadvertently lures believers into the company of these evil beings, which directly conflicts with their devotion to the true God.

Paul's plea to escape idolatry comes from a genuine concern for preserving the believer's spiritual connection with God. He aims to shield the Corinthians from harmful spiritual influences, guiding them toward a pure, untainted relationship with God.

To sum it up, Paul's main point in this passage is to emphasize discernment and caution against the risks of idolatry. While idols have no real power, idol worship leads to associating with demons. As such, believers should distance themselves from such practices and focus solely on nurturing an intense, exclusive bond with God.

> [14]*Therefore, my beloved, flee from idolatry.* [15]*I speak as to wise men; judge for yourselves what I say...* [19]*What am I saying then? That an idol is anything, or what is offered to idols is anything?* [20]*Rather, that the things which the Gentiles sacrifice they sacrifice to demons and not to God, and I do not want you to have fellowship with demons.* [21]*You cannot drink the cup of the Lord and the cup of demons; you cannot partake of the Lord's Table and of the table of demons.*
>
> (New King James Version, I Corinthians 10:14-15, 19, 21)

During his mission to the Gentiles, Paul shared Yeshua's testimony with his followers, admitting his vulnerabilities, such as fear and trembling. In 2nd Timothy, he recounts how the Lord offered him strength and support to spread the message to the Gentiles fully. Ephesus was a bustling metropolis during Paul's time, serving as the Greco-Roman Empire's second-largest city and a significant trade hub. Its prime location near the Cayster River-mouth enhanced its economic and military importance. At the same time, its majestic Temple of Diana

(Artemis) earned it a spot among the Seven Wonders of the Ancient World.

However, Ephesus wasn't without its troubles. Paul's teachings collided with Roman pagan beliefs. As Christianity flourished in the region, many were influenced to renounce their allegiance to these demonic spirits that had once brought them prosperity. Paul boldly labeled these entities as hostile spiritual forces, irritating officials. He urged fellow Christians to steer clear of these demonic powers.

> *[10]Finally, my brethren, be strong in the Lord and in the power of His might. [11]Put on the whole armor of God that you may be able to stand against the wiles of the devil.*
> *[12]For we do not wrestle against flesh and blood, but against principalities, against powers, against the rulers of the darkness of this age, against spiritual hosts of wickedness in heavenly places.*
>
> *(New King James Version, Ephesians 6:10-12)*

And;

> *[1]Now the Spirit [sic] expressly says that in latter times some will depart from the faith, giving heed to deceiving spirits and doctrines of demons, [2]speaking lies in hypocrisy, having their own conscience seared with hot iron.*
>
> *(New King James Version, 1 Timothy 4:1-2)*

The Gospel of Luke mentions that Paul held an important position in the temple during Jesus' crucifixion. Known as Saul at the time, he oversaw Stephen's execution and participated in arresting John and Peter. He dutifully fulfilled out his tasks, with strong support from Roman authority. However, on the way to Damascus, where he planned to capture Christ's followers, Paul encountered a life-changing experience. As he neared the city, a radiant light from heaven engulfed him, causing blindness. He fell face-first to the ground and heard a voice questioning why he was persecuting them.

In 2nd Thessalonians chapter 2, Paul elaborated that Satan's true nature would only be exposed when people's quest for truth surpassed their evil desires. Some would see this as a sinister display of prejudice chosen for financial stability.

> *³Let not one deceive you by any means; for that Day will not come unless the falling away comes first, and the man of sin is revealed, the son of Perdition, ⁴who opposes and exalts himself above all that is called God or that is worshipped, so that he sits as God in the temple of God, showing himself that he is God.*
>
> *(New King James Version, 2ⁿᵈ Thessalonians 2: 3-4)*

CHAPTER TWELVE

The Final Call: America's Caste System and the Quest for Liberation

L iberation from Satan's allure is crucial as our society continues on a path of rapid decline and deterioration. The intriguing aspect of racial equality between Black and white people is that it was never designed to be equal. While Blacks fought for their freedom and civil rights, whites effortlessly built wealth without interference from the governing authorities. True independence has always come at the cost of sweat, blood, and tears for Black individuals. This arduous journey has involved immense suffering in the face of bullets and lives lost to escape raging infernos. The battle was genuine in the quest to free the nation from institutional injustices and the sinister caste system. Unfortunately, that goal remains elusive as we grapple with oppression and inequality.

The unyielding greed and division within our society act as a malignant disease, distorting the heart of America and justifying its insatiable desires. Endless conflicts, zealous corporations, and self-absorbed politicians have usurped our worldview. The American hierarchical structure has always had deep-rooted connections with casteism and a tendency to obscure historical suffering. Generations of inequality and redlining policies have fostered thriving white communities while simultaneously hindering progress in Black and brown neighborhoods.

Residing in redlined communities feels like an unrelenting trap, perpetuating endless poverty cycles due to governmental policies that favor affluent neighborhood schools while allocating fewer funds to areas densely populated by minorities. Ironically, the same people condemn affirmative action for being meant to provide chances for minorities in businesses and educational institutions that have always been available to white individuals. In reality, white women benefit the most from affirmative action, nearly at double the rate of African Americans.

Concurrently, people of color continue to be overlooked regarding judicial and economic fairness. Protests against police brutality have become a global phenomenon, ignited by incidents such as George Floyd's death at the hands of white officer Derek Chauvin, who knelt on his neck until he became motionless. This gruesome incident led to a vast public outcry against the Minneapolis Police Department. Crowds took to the streets across America's major cities, chanting, "No justice, no peace." Mr. Floyd's killing was tragically not an unusual incident; it occurred soon after Ahmaud Arbery was slain while running by vigilantes and Breonna Taylor, a young EMT worker, was shot dead in her own house during a no-knock raid in Louisville, Kentucky. Disturbingly similar cases underline the pervading injustice in America.

These appalling injustices are brought to light as America wrestles with comprehending and tackling them in a suffocating caste system. The threat of unreliable informers is as significant as that of corrupt police officers. Both groups hold a certain degree of power and trust within their realms. Informers, who usually collaborate with law enforcement, give crucial insights into criminal activities, whereas police officers enforce the law, keep the peace, and safeguard communities.

However, when these people misuse their power, the results can be devastating. Untrustworthy informers could skew the data they offer, presenting false testimonies or concocting evidence—ultimately leading to wrongful detentions, convictions, and miscarriages of justice. Various motives can drive their actions, ranging from personal grudges to pursuits of financial gains or leniency in their criminal cases. Additionally, the common denominator between dishonest informers and corrupt cops lies in their potential abuse of authority, which undermines the justice system's integrity and erodes public trust. Additionally, the murder of African-Americans by white Americans can be viewed as a terrifying and deeply-rooted injustice intertwined with America's core issue of systemic racism. The nation's framework is rife with white privilege, permeating everything from the justice and economic systems to religious institutions.

In the United States, many seem oblivious to the concealed aspects of casteism, which corrodes every facet it touches. This caste system interweaves with institutionalized religion and has infiltrated our societal, economic, and political foundations. Its cruel intent was to subjugate Black and brown individuals based on their physical appearance while exalting whiteness. At the core of most white supremacists lies an ambition to dictate the rules by dominating the game of human worth without granting any fairness or respect to Black or brown people.

Since its inception, America has embraced white supremacy, effortlessly interweaving it into the fabric of past and present society. The main obstacle holding America back from thriving politically and economically is its unwillingness to face the hidden truths within white privilege. The nation's foundation was modeled after the Roman Empire in its adoration of whiteness.

The hidden force of white supremacy can no longer be overlooked. Like a lingering tremor after a massive wave, racism continues to plague our nation. As the tidal surge subsides, the potent disruption beneath the seafloor spreads into communities from every angle, hurling debris that endangers the core of our structures. America's foundation is crumbling due to our leaders' tiptoeing around systemic racism. They avoid addressing the root cause that is tearing apart the very essence of our country.

The deep-seated prevalence of systemic and structural racism in our laws and policies fuels white supremacy. Both systemic racism and colorism contribute to discriminatory behavior, stemming from long-standing beliefs that darker skin represents wickedness while lighter skin tones deserve special treatment. Racism's impact has made colorism a global issue, even infiltrating Africa. Despite the years since colonialism, skin color-based segregation still lingers. It's perplexing that in a continent primarily comprised of dark-skinned individuals, colorism remains an issue. Phrases like "You're too dark; you should bleach your skin" are casually tossed on social media. Meanwhile, organic skincare companies emerge, claiming to help black skin achieve a glow as if its natural melanin isn't radiant enough.

Segregation is at its worst in the entertainment industry, particularly in Africa. Numerous producers opt to work with lighter-skinned actresses, believing that fair skin equates to beauty and will draw larger audiences to their movies. Evidence of this lies in decade-old photos of actors who have visibly altered their complexions through bleaching. Posting a throwback photograph emphasizes the striking difference. Derogatory comments like "Your black is dirty" only exacerbate the issue, but when did black become synonymous with filth or ugliness? It's a remnant from colonial times that carries on till today.

The primary contributors to ongoing racism and colorism are deeply rooted in our society. This leads to mothers resorting to lightening their children's skin tones, hoping they'll grow up more attractive and ignoring that skin cancer can be fatal. Why allow external opinions about inferiority or civilization to define us when Africa is the cradle of life? In reality, altering skin color will not result in acceptance into the desired social circles.

A documentary named "Skin" showcased the negative consequences of skin bleaching. The interviewed subjects who had undergone the process expressed nothing but regret over their decisions. Instead of gaining wealth or status, they suffered from adverse effects and remorse. Before tackling the bleaching epidemic, we must confront the root causes: racism and white supremacy. Without these injustices, individuals would not be urged to jeopardize their well-being by modifying their appearances.

Simply put, the American Constitution is ink on paper. Jim Crow laws in the South were dangerously similar to slavery, allowing unlimited authority to those who oppose it. Apartheid and segregation aimed to segregate Blacks and whites while restricting Blacks' access to public amenities, equal housing opportunities, and decent jobs. White people ensured their dominance and influence remained intact throughout the social hierarchy, preserving their power in every aspect. Since America's inception, the caste system has been instrumental in maintaining elite bloodlines and establishing barriers to keep lower castes at the bottom of the economic ladder.

In India's past, interacting with or touching an Untouchable or Shudra was prohibited. The caste system stigmatized untouchables due to their darker skin pigmentation. An individual from the lowest caste was considered impure, requiring rituals for higher castes to avoid contamination. Bollywood movies are a prime example of this underrepresentation – dark-skinned Indians rarely have a screen presence. When portraying a dark-skinned character from a disadvantaged background, producers often hire non-black actors and temporarily darken their skin. One such example is the 2019 Bollywood film Bala, which received much backlash not only because it featured a dark-skinned protagonist from a low-income background but also because they hired Bhumi Pednekar, an actress with lighter skin color, for the role and temporarily darkened her complexion.

In India, the popularity of skin-lightening creams is growing, fueled by well-known celebrities endorsing these products. Dark-skinned individuals are often seen as less attractive and placed at the bottom of the racial hierarchy, leading to the belief that lighter skin equals a higher social standing. This trend is also evident in the entertainment industry in India and Africa. To secure roles in Bollywood, many aspiring actors undergo unnecessary procedures to lighten their skin. The industry prefers to cast light-skinned actors and alter their appearance as needed instead of hiring darker-skinned individuals. This discriminatory practice perpetuates the impact of white supremacy.

Black communities worldwide are striving for recognition of their struggles and equal treatment under the law. They continue to protest against racial injustice despite seemingly little progress. How long will they have to fight for fairness and humanity? How often must they plead to end violence based on skin color? When will society address the devastating consequences of racism? Black women often cannot wear their natural hair in corporate settings because it's deemed "unprofessional." To fit into the workforce's expectations, they must straighten their hair or wear hairpieces that resemble Western styles. Despite holding degrees from prestigious institutions, their natural hair is considered unprofessional due to white supremacy's influence. The global standard, unfortunately, leans heavily towards white features – from skin color to hairstyles.

For many years, Black individuals were forced to step aside onto grass or sand, letting white people walk on public sidewalks, with any eye contact being strictly prohibited. The foundations of our democracy only became a reality when Black people fought for their rights through great sacrifices on the streets of America. To grasp the concept of social stratification, one must understand its connection to the four-tier caste system of nobility: religious leaders and intellectuals, rulers and warriors, landowners and traders, and servants and peasants. At the lower end of this caste system were the shudra (dark-skinned Natives) and the untouchables. These outcasts often suffered from colorism, being deemed too Black to fit in with the rest of society.

The Western world embraced the most nefarious aspects of the Aryan caste system in its purest form. White supremacy refers to a mindset that seeks to dominate or subjugate anyone who is not white –mentally or physically. It has long been an opportunity for Europeans to exploit Native Americans and Africans, forcing them to work so that Europeans could enjoy a comfortable life. Although Africans performed most of the labor, lining European pockets with revenue while allowing them control over the land. White supremacy aims to manipulate information and warp culture through historical misrepresentation. Stereotypes based on misinformation have heightened these differences and given way to malicious intentions worldwide.

Eurocentrism thrives on unreflective critique. The colonial rulers and enslavers fostered a self-centered belief that demanded constant care in their homes or labor from dawn till dusk while depriving Africans of freedom. Working tirelessly in sweltering heat on cotton fields or sugar plantations was considered just another day of stealing free labor. Europeans devised cunning methods to siphon Africa's wealth into Western economies. Controlling every piece of publicity about Africa required manipulation through information channels and political strategies, ensuring a steady flow of wealth and continuous exploitation of Africa's labor force in the Western world.

In the book of Mathew, Yeshua describes a time after the tribulation that will lead to His return to earth:

> [29]*Immediately after the tribulation of those days the sun will be darkened, and the moon will not give its light; the stars will fall from heavens, and the powers in the heavens will be shaken.*
> [30]*Then the sign of the Son of Man will appear in heaven, and then all the tribes of the earth will mourn, and they will see the Son of Man coming on the clouds of heavens with power and great glory.* [31]*He will send His angels with a great sound of a trumpet, and they will gather together His elect from the four winds,*
> *from one end of heaven to the other.*
>
> *(New King James Version, Mathew 24:29-31)*

GOD'S JUDGMENT AND THE YOUTHFUL NATION

In the final days, Mysterious Babylon will rise to become the world's wealthiest and most powerful nation, only to face God's judgment. As the end times approach, the Antichrist will unleash plagues upon this enigmatic nation. Jeremiah foresaw the meteoric ascent of Mysterious Babylon and its swift downfall. Notably, this formidable nation will be youthful and inexperienced.

> *[45]My people go out of the midst of her! And let everyone deliver himself from the fierce anger of the Lord. [50]You who have escaped the sword, Get away! Do not stand still! Though Babylon was to mount up to heaven, and though she was to fortify the height of her strength, 53…yet from Me plunders would come to her.*
>
> *(New King James Version, Jeremiah 51:45, 50, 53)*

Satan cunningly disguises himself as an angel of light for those seeking to profit from his wicked actions. This trickery leads to unimaginable brutality and violence against anyone who challenges the notion of white supremacy. At its core, casteism deeply erodes human behavior, leading back to the fundamental sin of disobedience.

The wise prophet Jeremiah penned powerful words about dismantling this insidious caste system, which has inflicted immense suffering upon the covenant between God and His people.

> *[7]"How awful that day will be!*
> *No other will be like it.*
> *It will be a time of trouble for Jacob,*
> *but he will be saved out of it.*
> *[8]In that day," declares the Lord Almighty,*
> *"I will break the yoke off their necks*
> *and will tear off their bonds;*
> *no longer will foreigners enslave them.*
> *[9] Instead, they will serve the Lord their God*
> *and David their king,*
> *whom I will raise up for them."*
>
> *(New King James Version, Jeremiah 30:7-9)*

In the second letter to Timothy, Paul passionately conveys how salvation is granted to those who earnestly seek the Lord. In humility, correcting those in opposition, if God perhaps will grant them repentance, so that they may know the truth, and comes to their senses and escape the devil's snare, having been taken captive by him to do his will. But know this, that in the last days, perilous times will come: For men will be lovers of themselves, lovers of money, boasters, proud, blasphemers, disobedient to parents, unthankful, unholy, unloving, unforgiving, slanders, without self-control, brutal, despisers of good, having a form of godliness but denying its power. And from such people turn away!

The end of imperialism and white supremacy is fast approaching. Everyone would have to face the consequences of their wicked actions one day. Freedom held immeasurable significance. The decision has always been clear: succumb to the oppressive caste system and its dominant power, or embrace the teachings of the Savior, who sought to provide balance and liberation for all. The devoted disciples bravely traversed the world, spreading the message of God's kingdom that would demolish separation caused by the loathsome caste divisions through the Messiah's selfless sacrifice. Paul's profound words echoed this powerful sentiment in his letter to the Romans. For I am not ashamed of the gospel of Christ, for it is the power of God to salvation for everyone who believes, for the Jews first and also for the Greeks...God's wrath is revealed from heaven against all ungodliness and unrighteousness of men who suppress the truth in unrighteousness.

In Ephesus, the locals cherished their majestic temple dedicated to the goddess Diana, who they believed descended directly from Zeus. Despite this claim, the unwavering apostle Paul refused to dilute his faith. Paul firmly believed Yahweh was the only true God worthy of all worship and devotion. You were once in darkness, but now you are light in the Lord. Walk as children of the light…All things exposed are made manifest by the light, for whatever makes manifest is light. Therefore, He says: "Awake, you who sleep, arise from the dead, and Christ will give you light." In Ephesians chapter two, Paul captivatingly conveys God's all-encompassing love and liberation from oppression.

> *¹¹Therefore, remember that you, once were Gentiles in the flesh…¹²that at that time you were without Christ, being aliens from the commonwealth of Israel and strangers from the covenants of promise, having no hope and without God in the world. ¹³But now in Christ Jesus you who has made both one, and has broken down wall [sic] of separation, ¹⁵having abolished in His flesh the enmity, that is, the law of commandments contained ordinances, so as to create in Himself one new man from the two, thus making peace, ¹⁶and that He might reconcile them both to God in one body through the cross, thereby putting to death the enmity. ¹⁷And He came and preached peace to you who were afar off and to those who were nearby. ¹⁸For through Him we both have access by one Spirit to the Father.*
>
> (New King James Version, Ephesians 2:11-18)

In Paul's initial correspondence with the Thessalonians, he vividly portrays Christ's return, drawing intriguing parallels to John's experiences and visions.

But I do not want you to be ignorant, brethren, concerning those who have fallen asleep, lest you sorrow as others who have no hope, for if we believe that Jesus died and rose again, even so, God will bring with Him those who sleep in Jesus. For this, we say to you that the word of the Lord will not precede those who are asleep.

[16] For the Lord Himself will descend from heaven with a cry, the voice of an archangel, and the sound of God's trumpet. And the dead in Christ will rise first. [17] Then we who remain alive shall be caught up with them in the clouds to meet the Lord in air. And thus, we shall always be with the Lord.

(New King James Version, 1 Thessalonians 4:16-17)

In the opening chapter of Revelation, John was immersed in a vivid vision that unveiled the culmination of our world as we perceive it. He was struck by the powerful sound of a trumpet, accompanied by a voice that resonated: "I am the Alpha and the Omega, the First and the Last; what you see, write in a book and send it to the seven churches in Asia." John turned in the direction of the voice and saw seven golden lampstands. John saw one like the appearance of Christ, clothed with a garment down to His feet. He stood amid the lampstand with a golden girdle around His chest.

This Holy One, John describes as "One like the Son of Man," had hair like wool and eyes like a flame of fire. His feet were like fine brass as if they had been burned in a furnace, and out of His mouth was a sharpened two-edged sword. When John saw the glorified appearance of Christ, he fainted (Revelation 1:10-16). With a gentle touch of His right hand, the Lord comforted John and urged him not to worry. He then revealed His true identity to him.

I am the First and the Last. I am He who lived and was dead and behold, and I am forever. And I have the keys of Hades and Death. Write down the things you have seen, the things which are, and the things which will occur after this.

In the fourth chapter of Revelation, John heard a voice saying, "Come up here, and I will show you things which must take place after this," he was immediately taken to heaven in the spirit. John saw one seated on the throne, holding a scroll with seven seals in His hand, but no one was worthy of opening the scroll. John began to weep because no one could open the scroll. One of the elders said to him, "Do not weep. Behold, the Lion of the tribe of Judah, the root of David, has prevailed to open the scroll and to loose its seven seals." John saw a lamb with seven horns and seven eyes standing among the elders. The lamb came forward and took the scroll out of the right hand of the one seated on the throne. Then, the lamb proceeded to open the first seal. The four living creatures called out to John in a thunderous voice, saying, "Come and see."

In his vision, John witnessed a figure mounted on a majestic white horse, adorned with a crown and armed with a bow. This empowered rider embarked on a mission to dominate the world. During this time, the beast would establish a currency and religious system that would discriminate based on physical appearance. Though some would stand against this unjust hierarchy, they would ultimately face dire consequences.

The International Monetary Fund (IMF) and the World Trade Organization (WTO) work hand in hand, creating frameworks that encourage reliance on the powerful US dollar. As it stands, Africa's financial system is heavily influenced by this single currency, which has led to unfortunate consequences for many African leaders who've tried to lessen this dependency.

The U.S. dollar is vital for many African nations, helping facilitate international transactions, investments, and entry into global financial markets. However, it's worth highlighting that these countries actively strive to diversify their foreign exchange reserves and minimize their reliance on a single currency. They're driving initiatives to boost regional integration and encourage trade in local currencies, ultimately lessening their dependence on the U.S. dollar. Moreover, ambitious projects like the African

Continental Free Trade Area (AfCFTA) aim to bolster intra-African commerce and fortify regional currencies.

As the revelation unfolded, Christ revealed to John the intriguing Four Horsemen of the Apocalypse. These supernatural figures were granted power over nations and would play a pivotal role in the impending judgment of humanity. Upon breaking the second seal, a rider emerged on a blazing red horse, wielding a mighty sword. This rider was granted the power to strip peace from the world. As the Lamb unveiled the third seal, a dark horse materialized with its bearer, who held a set of scales in his hand. John then perceived a voice among the four living creatures, proclaiming, "A quart of wheat for a denarius and three quarts of barley for a denarius; yet spare the oil and wine" (Revelation 6:1-6).

As the fourth seal was unveiled, a mysterious rider emerged on a ghostly horse. Given the power to eliminate a quarter of humanity, the rider led his followers straight to hell's gates. When Christ revealed the fifth seal, John witnessed the souls of those sacrificed for embracing God's Word and Christ's testimony. Crying out in unison, they desperately asked, "How long, O Lord, holy and true, until You deliver justice and avenge our blood upon those who inhabit the earth?" The tragic depopulation of Africa impacted over 100 million individuals, with 30 million forced into slavery. Shockingly, an additional 70 million faced death as captives in the cruel Atlantic Slave Trade.

The caste system often called the mark of the beast, infiltrated European Capitalism – a monetary structure that amasses wealth through the production and private distribution of goods for trading. White settlers exclusively benefited from the market's freedom, resulting in prosperity for individuals and businesses based on race alone. This led to an exploitation of Africa's resources and those in both Americas, enriching white

Anglo-Saxons while causing instability in Africa and wiping out most of America's Indigenous populations.

A huge earthquake occurred as Christ opened the sixth seal, turning the sun black and the moon's blood crimson. Amidst this celestial turmoil, heaven quaked, and the sky rolled back upon itself. Every mountain and island shifted from their original positions, ultimately revealing the Grand Throne of God. Humanity now faced overwhelming fear as divine radiance enveloped their world. "Fall on us and hide us from the face of Him who sits on the throne and from the wrath of the Lamb[sic]...For the great day of His wrath has come, and who can stand?"

As the seventh seal opened, an eerie silence filled the air. John observed seven angels, each holding a trumpet, standing before God. A star plummeted from the heavens when the fifth angel blew its trumpet. This angel received the key to a bottomless pit, which unleashed a thick, dark smoke that obscured the sun and sky. From within the smoke emerged locusts with human faces, ready for battle. They donned iron armor, and their wings emitted sounds reminiscent of horse-drawn chariots charging into combat. These fearsome creatures were granted the power to torment humanity for five months (Revelation 9:1-5). John sought to convey these prophetic visions using language and imagery familiar to his first-century audience. However, it becomes evident that his visions were intended for the end times. John's depictions of chariots with wings probably refer to current tanks and fighter planes in combat.

The sixth angel played its trumpet, followed by a voice emanating from the four horns of a golden altar near God. This angel was instructed to free four outcast angels bound at the Euphrates River – allowing them to eliminate a third of humanity. In this vision, a vast army of two hundred million mounted soldiers materialized before John's eyes. Nose art predominantly adorns military aircraft, much like engraved animal illustrations on naval ships. John couldn't shake the image of these animal-like soldiers as the militias unleashed their fury in the warzone. The horseback riders raced on horseback, their steeds with lion-like heads spouting fire and brimstone with every breath, decked out in brilliant red, hyacinth blue, and yellow sulfur armor. These formidable horses possessed the power to wreak havoc on humanity, causing plagues with each exhale. The results were catastrophic: bombs and missiles rained from the sky, setting everything ablaze.

Despite this, humankind remained unrepentant. Rather than learning from their errors, the affluent and powerful descended even deeper into depravity, their souls devoid of compassion.

[20]But the rest of mankind, who were not killed by these plagues, did not repent of the works of their hands, that they should not worship demons, and idols of gold, silver, brass, stone and wood...[21]and they did not repent of their murders or their sorceries or their sexual immorality or their thefts.

(New King James Version, Revelation 9: 20-21)

The intense turmoil seemed like a message from the skies, meant to capture everyone's focus. John gazed upward, his eyes wide with amazement: I saw still another mighty angel coming down from heaven, clothed with a cloud. And a rainbow was on his head; his face was like the sun, and his feet like pillars of fire. He had a little book open in his hand. And he set his right foot on the sea and his left foot on the land, and cried loudly, as when a lion roar. When he cried out, seven thunders uttered their voices. "Now when the seven thunders uttered their voices,

I was about to write; but I heard a voice from heaven saying to me, 'Seal up the things which the seven thunders uttered, and do not write them.'"

While on the mystical island of Patmos, John experienced a vivid vision that swept him off his feet. He saw a terrifying beast emerge from the ocean, adorned with seven heads, ten horns, and ten crowns. This enigmatic creature had a sacrilegious name inscribed on its head and resembled a leopard with bear-like feet. Its mouth was akin to that of a lion, and it received immense power, along with a throne and great authority, from the dragon (Rev 13:1-3).

The beast was granted the ability to speak, uttering grandiose statements with blasphemy against God. It exercised its authority for 42 months. The four frightening beasts from Daniel's visions now stood united, ruling through a vicious system of supremacy. This wicked hierarchy ruthlessly persecuted anyone who refused to obey its commands. Consequently, it became Satan's instrument in his ongoing spiritual warfare against God's children.

The sinister system of oppression aims to keep humanity in constant conflict. Such superiority mindsets are deeply rooted in the unspoken caste hierarchy. For some, escaping caste discrimination is unimaginable. In the scriptures, Christ advised a wealthy man to sell his belongings, donate the proceeds to the poor, and secure his heavenly treasure. However, the man chose to stay bound by his worldly possessions. Unlike him, Abraham was also wealthy but never let his riches distance him from God or embrace a caste hierarchy for control. Abraham trusted God.

The corrupt caste system transcends all religious beliefs, aligning itself with demonic forces beyond our realm. This worldly construct entwines itself within all religious, political, and economic systems. It's thought that over 90% of global violence stems from the insidious influence of the caste hierarchy.

At its core, the caste system fuels countless wars across the globe and endangers our very existence. Many of the world's socioeconomic issues can be traced back to this corrupted structure. During the American Civil Rights Movement, citizens faced unimaginable horrors like being sprayed with fire hoses, brutal beatings, and lynchings in their pursuit of dismantling the oppressive caste system. It's hard to fathom how deeply ingrained loyalty to one's caste can be, even superseding love for family or country. In this context, the American flag and patriotism may hold little significance for those embracing casteism.

An insidious evil permeates America's fabric, stemming from the original sin of slavery. It feels like evil forces in the universe have tainted the nation. High-caste elites collaborate with lower-caste white individuals to control and suppress anyone they deem inferior. This complex caste structure perpetuates a hierarchy based on whiteness; the darker one's complexion or lower their caste, the greater their subjugation by dominant white caste members.

This explains humans' harshness towards each other, as they rely on their castes to shield them from retribution by granting the higher castes ultimate authority. What led our world to embrace such malevolence? In the final days, the caste system will be compelled to confront its fate, recognizing the atrocities it has inflicted upon humanity. The same spiritual loyalty initially introduced by the cast-out angels must relinquish its hold once people triumph over this deep-rooted mindset.

> *[18]For the wrath of God is revealed from heaven against all ungodliness men who suppress the truth in unrighteousness...[24]Therefore God also gave them up to uncleanness, in lusts of their hearts, to dishonor their bodies among themselves, [25]who exchanged the truth for a lie, and worshipped and served the creature rather than the Creator.*
>
> *(New King James Version, Romans 1:18, 24, 25)*

In Chapter 2 of Daniel, the Bible describes the fourth kingdom as powerful like iron, yet partly delicate. Daniel saw this as a mix of iron and ceramic clay that came together but failed to truly unite. The iron, clay, bronze, silver, and gold were all smashed into pieces and blown away by the wind. Ultimately, the mighty Roman Empire fell due to this ruling system's flaws, eventually crumbling apart.

> *[7]Authority was given to him over every tribe, tongue and nation ...[11]Then I saw another beast coming up out of the earth, and he had two horns like a lamb and spoke like a dragon. [12]And he exercises all the authority of the first beast in his presence and causes the earth and those who dwell in it to worship the first beast, whose deadly wound was healed.*
>
> (New King James Version, Revelation 13:7, 11, 12)

The final beast system, commonly known as the Whore of Babylon, is believed to be a rebirth of Rome, possessing all the characteristics of the ancient Assyro-Babylonian Empire. This enigmatic beast is a master of warfare, and John envisioned it unleashing fire from the sky upon its adversaries. Since state-of-the-art aircraft didn't exist during John's time, he shared his vision through words that best depicted what he had seen.

13He performs great signs, so that he even makes fire comes down from heaven on the earth in the sight of men. 14And he deceives those who dwell on the earth by those signs which he was granted to do in the sight of the beast, telling those who dwell on the earth to make an image to the beast who was wounded by the sword and lived.

(New King James Version, Revelation 13:13-14)

This enigmatic creature will seize control over global politics and commerce during its rule, making it impossible for anyone to conduct significant transactions without recognizing the Eighth Beast. This powerful entity will assume a vital, centralized position, placing it at the forefront of human society. The nation gained an outstanding bureaucracy and wealth, rendering it invulnerable to external forces. Its contribution to world affairs was regarded as divine.

In Revelation's thirteenth chapter, John witnessed the birth of this final beast system emerging from the earth. The system suffered greatly but eventually healed its wounds. In America's early history, the Civil War threatened to shatter the nation due to irreparable divisions that caused unrivaled casualties compared to other conflicts in its past. Though the Civil War left America battered, it persevered and grew into one of the most powerful nations in history. To unravel the enigma of the beast in Revelation, let's journey back to Daniel's four beasts to pinpoint the root of their power. It's plausible that their might stems from the ancient Vedas scriptures. The Hindu Vedas hold the key to embedding the caste system as an unshakable societal control mechanism. Such nations, dubbed as beasts, willingly embrace this revered doctrine. A hierarchical system seeped into these earthly realms' economic, commercial, and political foundations. Cunning tactics of social and human segregation based on race and privilege were employed to preserve dominance. The insidious impact of the caste system remains vastly undiscovered, and humanity seems oblivious to the profound depths of this dark predicament. What kind of force could unleash plagues upon Mysterious Babylon?

In ancient times, the Aryan Gentiles were said to have formed a pact with fallen angels, as described in the Vedas. Some experts think the caste system could represent the beast's mark, while others argue that the Roman Catholic Church, crafted from pottery clay, might be the actual mark. The papacy governed through a blend of church and state power, leading to the massacre of countless Black individuals in Africa and spreading hate worldwide.

This infamous, elitist system – the Anti-Christ – held sway over the Roman Church's papacy. It granted segments of the collapsed Roman Empire and American colonies (Rome's toes) authority to execute mass killings based on color prejudice. Regardless of how we perceive this situation, it's evident that people of color endured numerous cruelties due to their differences. Eventually, the Prince of Darkness will persuade humanity that inflicting violence and harm is necessary for our collective well-being.

Charles Darwin's concept of survival of the fittest inadvertently led to a brutal genocide against Australia's Aboriginal people, nearly causing their extinction. Women and children were captured and exploited as maids, cooks, and even sexual concubines to satisfy European desires and this dark period, known as the Black War, marked the mass murder of Tasmanian Aborigines by European settlers in the early 1800s. During British colonization, Indigenous Australians were forced from their homes and lands to live on an isolated island in the Bass Straits. They were oppressed under a strict caste system, kept uneducated, and required government permission for marriage or basic life necessities.

> *16He causes all, both small and great, rich and poor, free and slave, to receive a mark on their right hand or on their forehead...18Here is wisdom. Let him who has understanding calculate the number of the beast, for it is the number of a man: His number is 666.*
>
> *(New King James Version, Rev 13: 16-18)*

Five years post-graduation from Cambridge University, where he studied theology, Darwin embarked on an eye-opening journey to Africa, Austria, and South America. This exploration led him to question the validity of the Genesis creation story.

In his work, "The Descent of Man," Darwin argued that African individuals were genetically closer to apes than other humans. Additionally, he aggressively argued that Indigenous Africans and Australians were tantamount to domesticated animals. The *Colonial Times* published a news article stating:

We make no pompous display of Philanthropy. We say this unequivocally SELF DEFENSE IS THE FIRST LAW OF NATURE. THE GOVERNMENT MUST REMOVE THE NATIVES—IF NOT, AND THEY WILL BE HUNTED DOWN LIKE WILD BEASTS AND DESTROYED.

The concept of the "mark of the beast" (the caste system) has long served to rationalize and justify prejudiced attitudes, violent behaviors, and oppressive actions based on skin color or ethnic background in places of worship and among their followers. This insidious belief system has taken root in countless hearts and minds, dictating aspects of their lives and occupations through adherence to a hierarchy of superiority.

In simpler terms, accepting institutional oppression or taking advantage of cultural and economic disparities means succumbing to the mark of the beast. The Aboriginal Australians lost their original language and culture due to Great Britain's (the seventh beast) deceitful actions. Many Aboriginal people faced torture, death, and the ransacking of their villages by European settlers. Mysterious Babylon is the eighth sinister beast in scripture, displaying cruelty akin to Great Britain and even surpassing the brutality of fallen Rome. Racism and intolerance continue to thrive in positions of power, with deplorable acts morphing but never ceasing. The blood-stained history and disgraceful actions brought upon by Mysterious Babylon are no longer hidden from view.

The fallen angels will unleash calamities upon enigmatic Babylon:

Because ye have said, We have made a covenant with death, and with hell are we at agreement; when the overflowing scourge shall pass through, it shall not come unto us: for we have made lies our refuge, and under falsehood have we hid. (Isaiah 28:15)

We would have healed Babylon, but she is not healed. Forsake her, and let us go everyone to his own country; For her judgment reaches heaven and is lifted to the skies…O you who dwell by many waters, abundant in treasures, your end has come. (Jeremiah 51:9-13)

In Revelation Chapter 16, John hears a commanding voice from the temple, instructing the seven angels to unleash God's wrath upon the earth through their bowls. The angels proceed to show John the condemnation of Babylon. As the first angel empties his bowl, odious sores are inflicted on those who bear the mark or worship the beast's image. The second and third angelic outpourings dispense retribution on oceans, rivers, and springs. They transform water into blood, causing every aquatic life form to perish. When the fourth angel directs his ire toward the sun, its intense heat scorches people to their core. Instead of showing remorse, they curse God and refuse to repent.

The sixth angel dries up the Euphrates River by discharging his wrath into it; this ominous act paves the way for Armageddon's epic battle. Revelation 17 intensifies as the scene shifts toward the impending doom of the great seductress. An angel who carries one of the seven bowls unveils to John how the harlot shall be punished for leading humanity astray into corruption and evil. Come, I will show you the judgment of the great harlot who sits on many water, with whom the kings of the earth committed fornication, and the inhabitants of the earth were made drunk with the wine of her fornication" (Revelation 17:1-2). John glimpsed a lady perched upon a vibrant red beast in the wild. She embodied the extravagant essence of the enigmatic Babylon, adorned with shimmering gold and priceless gems. Her beautiful pearls caught John's attention as she held a golden chalice filled with unspeakable horrors. Emblazoned on her brow was a name:

MYSTERY, BABYLON THE GREAT, THE MOTHER OF HARLOTS AND THE ABOMINATIONS OF THE EARTH."

The angel revealed the mystery of the vision after John seemed to be surprised:

> [7]*But the angel said to me, "Why did you marvel? I will tell you the mystery of the woman and of the beast that carries her, which has seven heads and ten horns. [8]The beast that you saw was, and is not, and will ascend out of the bottomless pit and go into perdition (hell)…[10]There are also seven kings. Five have fallen, one is, and the other has not yet come. And when he comes, he must continue for a short time. [11]The beast that was, and is not, is himself also the eight, and is of the seven.*
>
> *(New King James Version, Revelation 17:7-11)*

An angel unveiled to John the future where Satan would deploy spiritual warfare against the Hebrews and their allies. In this conflict, Gentile kingdoms, known as the beast, would aid Satan's deceptive assault on those refusing his reign. They would rely on their military, economic, and political prowess rather than trust in God's supreme power. While on Patmos Island, the angel informed John that "Five kingdoms had fallen; one is, and the other has not yet come." By this time, the Assyrians, Babylonians, Medes, Persians, and Greeks had all succumbed to defeat. Although this particular angel didn't name the seventh empire, it emphasized the eighth beast: Mysterious Babylon.

During John's lifetime, Rome was the powerful Gentile kingdom and was considered the sixth beast in his vision. As Rome fell, the British inherited much of its power. With Britain emerging as the largest inheritor of Rome's fallen empire, the old Roman Empire's seven powers invaded Africa. In Revelation 19, John witnessed the capture of the beast and false prophet before they were hurled into a fiery lake of burning brimstone. The twentieth chapter saw an angel descending from heaven with a key to a bottomless pit and a great chain in hand. The angel then seized and imprisoned Satan in this pit for a millennium. John also observed the souls of Christ's witnesses; they were resurrected to rule with him for 1,000 years while others remained dead.

As foretold in Ezekiel 39 and Revelation 20, Gog and Magog would launch an immense assault against Israel. This event likely happens after Satan's 1,000-year imprisonment ends and he is set free. In Cyrus' third year as king, Daniel underwent a three-week fast which preceded his fourth divine vision, similar to John's revelation. On the first month's twenty-fourth day, while strolling along the Tigris Riverbanks, Daniel glanced upwards to see a vision of a man dressed in linen with a gold belt encircling his waist.

The Bible reveals that countless people will be drawn towards the rule of evil, comparable to grains of sand by the seashore. During the peak of ancient Rome's authority, several African nations contributed to Rome's victories against its adversaries. Consequently, Ethiopia and Libya, two African countries, were identified as potential allies of the North to fight against Israel due to the resurgence of Gog and Magog. Despite this alliance, God will overcome these African nations and those from the North.

The burying of the dead from this devastating conflict will last seven months. Divine fire will not only obliterate Gog and Magog but also wipe out Persian, Ethiopian, and Libyan soldiers positioned in Israel's mountains alongside forces from the North. Nevertheless, those residing in the southern lands will be spared. Since this combined force was led by Magog (the North) and Satan, God will ultimately eliminate the root of this evil by destroying Magog, Gog, and Satan: And I will send fire on Magog and those who dwell securely in the coastlands; then they shall know that I am the Lord. (Ezekiel 39:1-6)

The devil who led them astray was thrown into a lake of fire and sulfur, joining the beast and false prophet already present there. (Revelation 20:10). His face shone like lightning, and his eyes blazed like fiery torches. His arms and legs resembled polished bronze, and his voice boomed like the sound of a great crowd. Daniel, overwhelmed, fell to the ground unconscious. Sensing this, the Angel touched him, reviving his strength. The Angel then spoke to Daniel:

¹²Do not fear, Daniel. For the first day that you set your heart to understand, and to humble yourself before your God, your words were heard, ¹³but the prince of the kingdom of Persia withstood me twenty-one days; and behold, Michael, one of the chief princes, came to help me…¹⁴Now I have come to make you understand what will happen to your people in the latter days,

for the vision refers to many days yet to come.

(New King James Version, Daniel 10: 12-14*)*

In Daniel's compelling vision, he offers a glimpse into a far-off future, detailing a sequence of events where various powerful forces emerge to rule the world. Following the decline of ancient Greece, Daniel saw the rise of a great yet unnamed empire wielding immense influence. As this new kingdom takes shape, it will break up and spread across the planet, but without the strength of previous rulers. The ascent of Rome from the remnants of Greece signaled its place as the fourth beast in Daniel's vision, dominating vast regions worldwide.

In an enthralling twist, the story unfolds in Daniel 11:5, where Ethiopia (symbolizing the South) gathers its strength to face Rome (the North), stopping Africa's total conquest. As the chapter starts, Ethiopia leads the southern resistance against Rome, displaying formidable power. But as Daniel predicted, Rome and Ethiopia ultimately lost their status as ruling forces in their regions.

In the book of Daniel, it reads:

¹⁵So the king of the North shall come and build a siege mound, and take a fortified city; and the forces of the South shall not withstand him. Even his choice troops shall have no strength to resist. ¹⁶But he who comes against him shall do according to his own will, and no one shall stand against him. He shall stand in the Glorious Land with destruction in his power.

(Daniel 11:15-16)

The North is set to launch a powerful attack on Egypt, causing Ethiopia and Libya to submit to its dominance. This could be due to the North's pride or fear as it regains its position as a global superpower. The North's unexpected power play against the South will secure essential resources. In its prime, Ethiopia had successfully defended itself against foes such as Assyria, Babylon, Persia, Greece, and Imperial Rome. Yet, as Daniel prophesied, Ethiopia eventually became submissive to the North. Nowadays, Ethiopia's global influence has waned due to widespread famine and war; however, there is potential for it to align with a Northern power in a military campaign against Israel: "He will gain control of the treasures of gold and silver and all the riches of Egypt, with the Libyans and Nubians in submission" (Daniel 11:43).

Daniel's twelfth chapter reveals his struggle to comprehend the enigma of ages: "But you, Daniel, shut up the words, and seal the book until the time of the end; many shall run to and from, and knowledge shall increase." He witnessed two men dressed in linen on either side of a riverbank while another hovered above the water. Curious, one linen-clad man addressed his airborne counterpart.

"How long shall the fulfillment of these wonders be?"

The man above the water answered and said, "That it shall be a time, times, and half a time; and the power of the holy people has been completely shattered, all these things shall be finished." Then Daniel asked, "My lord, what shall be the end of these things?"

The Lord replied, "Go your way, Daniel, for the words are closed and sealed till the end." In the forty-seventh chapter, Ezekiel returned to see freshly flowing water under the temple. On the river bank, there were many trees on each side. The trees produced abundant fruit, and the leaves were used for medicine.

Then the angel said to Ezekiel, "This water flows toward the eastern region, goes down into the valley, and enters the sea. When it reaches the sea, its waters are healed. And it shall be that every living thing that moves, wherever the rivers go, will live." In Revelation's twenty-first chapter, John witnessed the sight of the holy city, New Jerusalem, descending from the heavens. This city did not need sunlight or moonlight as God's glory radiated throughout, illuminating every corner. Only those in the Book of Life could call this sacred place home. Interestingly, John's visions and allegorical descriptions share striking similarities with what Ezekiel saw approximately six centuries earlier.

> *¹And he showed me a pure river of water of life, clear as crystal, proceeding from the throne of God and of the Lamb. ²In the middle of its street, and on either side of the river, was a tree of life, which bore twelve fruits, each tree yielding its fruit every month. The leaves of the tree were for the healing of the nations. ³And there shall be no more curses, but the throne of God and of the Lamb shall be in it, and His servants shall serve Him. ⁴They shall see His face, and His name shall be on their foreheads.*
>
> *(New King James Version,* Revelations 22:1-4)

Zechariah urged the people to repent and return to the Lord, emphasizing the importance of reconstructing God's Temple. He assured them that this would lead to greater prosperity for the Israelites. Through his night visions, Zechariah saw a new era approaching in which the Lord would fight their battles and bring back all those who had been dispersed, reuniting them in Zion.

Shout, O daughter of Jerusalem! Behold, your King is Coming to you; He is just and having salvation, lowly and riding on a donkey, A colt, the foal of a donkey.

Conclusion

Wow, what a fantastic journey we've been on! After over 200 pages exploring the past, present, and future, delving into sacred texts, we've finally concluded this book. Along the way, we've investigated racism, end times, and various aspects of evil that permeate society. Interestingly enough, these harmful practices of discrimination and wickedness did not begin in the 21st century – they have been present since ancient times when people turned their backs on God to serve other idols, leading to the troubling issues we face today.

Unfortunately, racism persists in our world, but we can strive to become better individuals. We must work towards being the best versions of ourselves. This book highlights how some white Christians acknowledged the evil of slavery and faced societal backlash for their stance. The core lesson is about accepting compassion, as shown by historical and biblical connections. Regardless of social status or skin color, it's crucial to abandon society's harmful norms that consider certain groups inferior and treat everyone equally.

Writing this book has been a rewarding experience for me. I hope it serves as an eye-opening revelation for you, unveiling the roots of discrimination and injustice. Thank you for reading my book, and remember to apply the valuable knowledge you've gained positively.

Cheers!

Bibliography

Aboriginal Tasmanian. (2003, June 5). Wikipedia. http://
en.wikipedia.org/wiki/Tasmanian_Aborigines

Adkins, L. and Adkins, R.A. (1994). *Handbook to Life in Ancient
Rome.* Oxford University

Press.
Africa Opposing Viewpoints. (2008). Greenhaven Press.*Alexander the
Great.* (n.d.). Carpenoctem. http://www.carpenoctem.tv/military/
alex.html

Ancient Civilization. (2000). Thinkquest. http://www.library.
thinkquest.org/C004203/science/science02.htm

Ancient Mother of the Sudan and Ethiopia. (n.d.). Suite 101. http://
www.suite101.com/content/queen-candace-of-antiquity-al67567

Ancient Nubia: Map and History of Rulers. (n.d.). http://wysinger.
homestead.com/mapofnubia.html

Anderson, S. (1995). *The Black Holocaust for Beginners.* Writer and
Readers Publishing, Inc.

Atlas of the Bible: An Illustrated Guide to the Holy Land. (1982).
Reader's Digest Association, Inc.

Babylon Empire. (n.d.). Livius. http://www.livius.org/ba-bd/babylon/
babylonian_empire.html

Benson, C. (1970). *Supernatural Dreams and Visions.* Logos International.

Bernstein, P. L. (2012). *The Power of Gold, The History of an Obsession.* John Wiley & Sons, Inc.

Bishop, A. & Dunston, J. (1993). *The Black Man in the Old Testament and Its World.*

Africa World Press, Inc.

Black War. (2004, February 27). Wikipedia. http://en.wikipedia.org/wiki/Black_War

Blight, D. *The Civil War and Reconstruction Era, 1845-1877: Lecture 10 Transcript.* Open Media. http://openmedia.yale.edu/projects/iphone/departments/hist/hist119/transcript10.html

Burton, K.A. (2007). *The Blessing of Africa.* InterVarsity Press.

Casson, L. (1981). *Treasures of the World, The Pharoahs.* Stonehenge Press, Inc.

Ciment, J. (2001). *Atlas of African-American History .* Media Projects Inc.

Civil Rights. (n.d.). Southern Connecticut State University. http://www.southernct.edu/~ils69315/sixties/civilrights.htm

Clarke, J.H. (1998). *Christopher Columbus and the Afrikan Holocaust Slavery and the Rise of European Capitalism.* A&B Publisher Group.

Costello, D. & Duvall, T. (2020, March 17). *How did Breonna Taylor die? What to know about the Louisville woman shot by police.* Courier Journal. https://www.courier-journal.com/story/news/local/2020/05/12/breonna-taylor-case-what-know-louisville-emt-killed-cops/3110066001/

Cummins, J. (2010). *The World's Bloodiest History: Massacre, Genocide, And Scars They left on*

Civilization. Fair Winds Press.

Darwin, C. (1998). *The Descent of Man.* Prometheus Books.

Dawood, N.J. (1995). *The Koran.* The Penguin Group.

Debroy, B.D. (2011). *The Holy Vedas: Rig Veda Yajur Veda Sama Veda Atharva Veda.* B.R. Publishing Corporation.

Dionysus or Bacchus. (n.d.). In Depth Info. http://www.indepthinfo.com

Duncan, M.J. (2003). *The Complete Idiot's Guide to African American History.* Pearson Education, Inc.

Dyer, C.H. (1995). *World News and Bible Prophecy.* Tyndale House Publishers.

Dyer, C.H. (2003). *The Rise of Babylon.* Moody Publishers.

Faal, C. *The Partition of Africa.*(2009, February 21). Black Past. http://www.blackpast.org/?q=gah/partition-africa

Fagg, J.E. (1965). *Cuba, Haiti, & The Dominican Republic.* Prentice-Hall, Inc.

Feldman, G. (1999). *Politics, Society, And the Klan in Alabama.* The University of Alabama Press.

Finley, M.I. (1965). *Josephus: The Jewish War and other selections.* Twayne Publishers, Inc.

Fraley, B. (1984). *The Last Days in America.* Christian Life Publishers.

Gaines, A. (1994). *Herodotus and the Explorers of the Classical Age.* Chelsea House Publishers.

Gelb, N. (2010). *Kings of the Jews*. The Jewish Publication Society.

Goddard, John.(2007, May 31). *Where Ancient Gods and Royalty Walked*. The Toronto Star. https://www.thestar.com/news/2007/05/31/where_ancient_gods_and_royalty_walked.htm

Greenwood, S. (2006). *The Encyclopedia of Magic Withchcraft*. Hermes House.

Griffith, R.T.H. (2008). *The Rig Veda Complete*. Forgotten Books.

Hart, G. (2000). *Ancient Egypt*. Dorling Kindersley.

Hawass, Z. (2005). *Tutankhamun and the Golden Age of the Pharoahs*. Geographic Society.

Hill, J. (2010). *Herodotus on Cambyses*. Ancient Egypt Online. http://www.ancientegyptonline.co.uk/HerodCambyses.html

Hillel, D. (2006). *The Natural History of the Bible*. Columbia University Press.

Hirsch, J.S. (2002). *Riot And Remembrance: The Tulsa Race War and Its Legacy*. Houghton Mifflin Company.

Hislop, R.A. (1959). *The Two Babylons*. Loizeaux Brothers, Inc.

Hitchcock, M. (1999). *The Complete Book of Bible Phophecy*. Tyndale House Publishers.

Hithcock, M. (2003). *The Second Coming of Babylon*. Multnomah Publishers, Inc.

Houston, D.D. (2007). *Wonderful Ethiopians of the Ancient Cushite Empire*. BiblioBazaar.

Jackson, J.G. (2001). *Introduction to African Civilizations*. Kensington Publishing Corp.

Jensen, I.L. (1981). *Jensen's Survey of the New Testament*. The Moody Bible Institute.

Jeremiah, D.D. (2010). *The Coming Economic Armageddon.* NavPress Publishing Group.

Jugurtha. (2002, December 13). Wikipedia. http://en.wikipedia.org/wiki/Jugurtha

Hazleton, L. (2007). *Jezebel, The Untold Story of the Bible's Harlot Queen.* Doubleday Broadway Publishing Group.

Herodotus. (1982). The Persian War, Shepherd, W. (Trans.). Cambridge University Press.

Karimi, F. (2020, August 28). *Kenosha shooting suspect called a friend to say he 'killed somebody,' police say, and then shot two others.* CNN. https://www.cnn.com/2020/08/28/us/kyle-rittenhouse-kenosha-shooting/index.html

Khan, S.M. (2007). *The Shallow Graves Of Rwanda.* I.B. Tauris Publishers.

Kosof, A. (1989). *The Civil Rights Movement and Its Legacy.* Franklin Watts.

Loewen, J.W. (2007). *Lies My Teacher Told Me, Everything Your American History* Textbook Got Wrong. The New Press.

Mark P.L. & Silberman, N.A. (1995). *Invisible America: Unearthing Our Hidden History.* Henry Holt and Company, Inc.

McKissack, P.A. (1987). *The Civil Rights Movement in America: from 1865 to the Present.* Regensteiner Publishing Enterprises, Inc.

Millmore, M. (2007). *Imagining Egypt.* Black Dog and Leventhal Publishers, Inc.

Napata. (2005, June 6). Wikipedia. http://en.wikipedia.org/wiki/Napata

Newton, John. (2010). *Thoughts Upon the African Slave Trade.* https://cowperandnewtonmuseum.org.uk/wp-content/uploads/2020/07/thoughts-upon-african-slave-trade-john-newton.pdf

Noss, D.S. (1999). *A History of the World's Religions 10th Edition .* Prentice-Hall, Inc.

One of Africa's best kept secrets.(n.d.). BBC. https://www.bbc.com/news/world-africa

Packard, J.M. *American Nightmare The History of Jim Crow.* New York: St. Martin's Press, 2002.

Packer, J.I. (1995). *Nelson's Illustrated Encyclopedia of Bible Facts.* Thomas Nelson, Inc.

Pike, A. (2010). *The Aryan Race: Country, Character, and Manners of The Indo-Aryans.* Kessinger Publishing.

Psamtik I. (2004, January 27). Wikipedia. http://en.wikipedia.org/wiki/Psamtik I

Punic Wars. (2001, October 17). Wikipedia. en.wikepedia.org/wiki/Punic_wars

Rediker, M. (2007). *The Slave Ship, A Human History.* Penguin Group, Inc.

Remembering Martin Luther King, Jr. (n.d.). Black Americans. http://www.blackamericans.com/black-history/black-history

Rodgers, N. (2006). *Ancient Rome.* Hermes House.

Roman Spain. (n.d.). Citytours Barcelonia. http://www.citytoursbarcelona.com/roman_spain.html

Sennacherib Prism. (n.d.). Bible Dudes. http://bibledudes.com/bilical-studies/finds/prism-translation.php

Sennacherib: the Year –701. (2012). Varchive. http://www.varchive.org/tac/701.htm

Slavery In Ancient Rome. (n.d.). Rich East. http://www.richeast.org/htwn/Greeks/Romans/slavery/slavery2.html/

Smith, R. & Jones, S.L. (2000). *The Prentice Hall Anthology of African American Literature.* Prentice Hall, Inc.

Spiegel, M. (1996). *The Dreaded Comparison: Human and Animal Slavery.* Mirror Books/I.D.E.A.

Spielvogel, J.J. (2005). *World History Modern Times.* National Geographic Society.

Splendors Of The Past: Lost Cities of the Ancient World. (1981). National Geographic Society.

Statue of Liberty. (2001, October 22). Wikipedia. http://en.wikipedia.org/wiki/Statue_of_Liberty

Tantamani. (2004, November 2). Wikipedia. http://en.wikipedia.org/wiki/Tantamani

Temple of Artemis. (2010). Ephesus. http://www.ephesus.ws/temple-of-artemis.html

The Carnival Celebration that Became Christmas & New Year's Eve. (n.d.). Saturnalia. http://www. carnaval.com/saturnalia

The Hanging Gardens of Babylon. (n.d.). Ocean Baby. http://www.ocean-baby.com/

The History of Herodotus. (n.d.). Classic MIT. http://classic.mit.edu/Herotodus/history.html

The Holy Bible, New King James Version. (1992). Thomas Nelson, Inc.

The Kushite conquest of Palenstine and the 'Assyro-Kushite Wars.' (n.d.) Ancient Sudan. http://www.ancientsudan.org/history_07_assyro. htm

The Urantia Book. (1995). Urantia Foundation.

The World Book Encyclopedia. (1991). World Book, Inc.

The World's Last Mysteries.(1981). Reader's Digest Association.

Third Punic War. (n.d.) UNRV Roman History. http://www.unrv. com/empire/third-punic-war.php

Wagman, R.J. (1993). *The Supreme Court: A Citizen's Guide.* Pharos Books.

Walvoord, J.F & Zuck, R.B. (1983). *Bible Knowledge Commentary: New Testament.* David C. Cook.

Wilson, A. (1997). *Paul: The Mind of the Apostle.* W.W. Norton & Company.

Windsor, R.R. (2003). *From Babylon to Timbuktu.* Windsor Golden Series.

Wintz, C.D. (2007). *Harlem Speaks: A Living History of the Harlem Renaissance.* Sourcebooks.

Youngblood, R.F., Bruce, F.F., Nelson, T. & Harrison, R.K. (1995). Nelson's New Illustrated Bible Dictionary. Thomas Nelson, Inc.